Colourful
HOUSEPLANTS
an illustrated guide to indoor gardening

Colourful
HOUSEPLANTS
an illustrated guide to indoor gardening

edited by
Peter McHoy & David Squire

octopus

Contents

First published 1978 by Octopus Books Limited 59, Grosvenor Street London W1

© 1978 Octopus Books Limited .. .. ISBN 0 7064 0706 7

Produced by Mandarin Publishers Limited, 22a, Westlands Road, Quarry Bay, Hong Kong.

Printed in Singapore

Introduction

Houseplants can bring the joy of gardening into every home – whether it is a modest flat in a high-rise tower or a country home with rambling garden. They also provide year-round interest and colour, often for a fairly modest outlay. Like most hobbies, however, the real challenges and rewards are not obvious until one becomes involved with it. Stalwarts though they are, the ubiquitous Busy-Lizzies and Rubber Plants do little justice to the wealth of wonderful plants waiting to be discovered.

Many houseplant enthusiasts start by purchasing a small range of subjects that catch their attention at a nursery or florist, and usually the collection grows quickly – often spurred on by the exchange of cuttings with friends. These general collections can be most attractive, but unless plenty of time is available to give each plant individual attention, their different needs can be very demanding. It is amazing how easily 50 or even 100 different species can be amassed in a year or two without even trying.

To make success more sure for the beginner, and to present challenges to the more experienced, all the plants described have been graded according to ease of cultivation – one star indicates an easy, tolerant plant, two-stars a more difficult that should thrive with attention; three-star plants are for the experienced grower. As with outdoor gardening, the serious houseplant enthusiast often tends to specialise – in ferns, cacti, flowering plants, or perhaps bromeliads or bulbs. That is the stage at which the more temperamental subjects can be attempted.

Foliage plants are perhaps the most frequently grown type of houseplant, and this is because most of the green-leaved plants we grow indoors can tolerate the poor lighting conditions, while still retaining good shape and growth, much better than the majority of flowering plants. But those with colourful foliage will usually have leaves of a much more intense shade if given a position in good light.

Palms and ferns deserve special mention because they are often neglected – yet they can make a superb centrepiece or focal point in a modern home. Although palms can grow quite large, one of the best to start with, *Chamaedorea elegans* the Parlour Palm, will only reach about 120cm (4ft) after many years.

Cacti and succulents have their own devoted following, and are to be recommended to anyone looking for trouble-free houseplants. Although summer watering should never be neglected, they will look after themselves during the holidays much more successfully than most other houseplants, and in the winter they need practically no attention and only a little warmth. It is perhaps only when a collection has been started that the sheer variety of shapes and forms captures the imagination. Cacti and succulents are far from lacking in colour either, for the Christmas and Easter Cacti can make a spectacular display. And once the plants become established, the summer-flowering desert kinds can produce quite breathtaking blooms.

Bromeliads tend to be more expensive to buy and are not easy to grow successfully over a long period; but some, such as *Billbergia nutans,* are worthy of a place in any home – this plant is easy to grow and its distinctive flowers marked with blue, green, yellow and pink, are very welcome in May and June.

Bulbs and corms do not usually spring to mind as high-priority houseplants, yet there is little to beat a well-grown bowl of full and fragrant hyacinths in the bleak winter months. But many more bulbs are worth considering – from the tiny and dainty blue and white Glory of the Snow (chionodoxa) to the massive Scarborough Lily (Vallota speciosa). Some lilies can also make interesting houseplants.

The chances are everyone who starts to explore the wonderful world of indoor plants will tend to specialise sooner or later – but the real joy of gardening comes from being prepared to try something new . . . to discover another previously unknown gem. We hope this book uncovers some of them for you.

Hippeastrum,

The right environment

Growing and displaying plants indoors has been popular for many generations. Particularly during the 17th, 18th and 19th centuries, people adorned their houses with exotic plants, and in some cases sponsored plant hunters to travel far afield to collect specimens for them. During the late 19th century interest in plants

waned, but about 20 years ago everything changed, and house plants became popular again in every walk of life, to an extent greater than ever before.

The purposes to which house plants are put, and the motives for possessing and caring for them, are manifold. Sometimes it is for their exceptional value in interior decor, which may or may not be inspired by an interest in growing them; then there is that almost primitive urge to cultivate, which exists in so many human beings, who derive satisfaction from bringing their gardening adventures, especially during the winter, into the comfortable environment of their homes; there are others who, haunted by a sense of deprivation because they have no garden, find that in house plants they can enjoy the interest they have yearned for; and, finally, there are the connoisseurs who find great joy in accepting the challenge that growing the more delicate and difficult subjects offers them.

Whatever the motivation, you will want to succeed, and there are a number of different aspects of cultivation and environment that have to be considered if house plants are to thrive.

Light
The fact is that human beings are able to remain healthy, or at least they think they can, in less light than plants need to thrive. Most places in our homes are not light enough to suit the well-being of many indoor plants, which means keeping them at their best under such conditions is not an easy task. It is, however, important to dispel one myth — most houseplants don't need long spells in direct sunshine; with a few exceptions, plants object to being exposed directly to the rays of the sun.

Dedicated enthusiasts can overcome the difficulty of poor lighting by installing cabinets or racks of shelves illuminated with fluorescent strip-lighting during the day (special tubes should be used which emit the right kind of light). A few gardeners even despise the unpredictable strength of natural light during the day and create a completely artificial environment for their house plants in a cellar, where the strength and duration of the light can be rigidly controlled.

Most of us are happy enough without special equipment, but the important lesson is that most house plants must have good light, but they appear to be as happy in artificial light as in sunlight.

The general rule is to put most plants in the lightest place out of prolonged sunshine in the room, and this usually means as near the window as possible. Obviously it helps to keep the curtains and blinds fully open as long as possible during the day. If house plants have to be put into a dark corner, make sure that suitable fluorescent lighting is provided to supplement the natural light. It must also be remembered that a group of plants in a dark corner is not very decorative unless it is lit up!

Warmth

Warmth is an obvious necessity, especially when one realizes the very warm climates from which many of our houseplants come. Fortunately many more houses have central heating nowadays and this is a great help, provided humidity is given.

The big menace is fluctuations of temperature arising from fairly long periods early in the day when rooms are not heated much, then other periods when they might be overheated, followed by a rapid fall in the temperature during the night, perhaps even below freezing point. Such conditions are far more damaging for most plants than being kept in a constantly cool place. So keep houseplants in a position where the temperature is as uniform as possible. Always avoid, for example, standing them on a mantelpiece or on a shelf over the radiator, where they might be roasted for part of the day, or behind closed curtains on the windowsill at night where it is likely to become intensely cold.

The A–Z sections in the following chapters list the minimum night temperature that should be maintained for each plant, so decide on the temperatures you feel able to maintain and choose your plants with this in mind.

There are no temperatures suggested for the bulbs, as most are hardy and are only brought indoors to flower. Those bulbs that do require specific temperatures are detailed.

Humidity

A good number of houseplants have a preference for high or moderate humidity. And as humidity is linked with temperature and air circulation excessive heat in a closed area will dry the atmosphere to such an extent that it is harmful to many plants. Controlling humidity in a living-room is difficult — if overdone some plants might revel in it, but human-beings won't.

Moist air is as important as warmth to many houseplants, so if success is to be attained it is necessary to provide humidity in the vicinity of the plants themselves. There are two principal ways in which this can be done. The first is to put the plant in its original pot in another rather larger one (which might well have a decorated exterior), and to pack the space on the bottom and sides with moist peat, kept continuously moist. The second is to use a pebble tray. This consists of a tray or dish half filled with pebbles on which the pot is stood. Water is added to nearly cover the stones. This is topped up from time to time to compensate for evaporation loss.

Some plants, such as *Cyclamen persicum* and saintpaulias, respond well to a periodic steam bath. This is given by placing an upturned seed pan or block of wood at the bottom of a washing-up bowl and pouring into it boiling water to a level just below the top of the pan or block. The pot is stood on this platform for five minutes and then returned to its usual quarters.

Syringing or spraying the foliage, particularly in hot weather, assists in maintaining a high level of humidity. It is best to syringe early in the day rather than late afternoon or evening when the temperature is beginning to fall.

Watering

Water is important to all plants, but it becomes more of a problem for plants in pots. The problem many houseplant owners have to face is *when* to water. Unfortunately there is no one simple answer, so much depends on the nature of the plant, the time of year and the environment. Plants with fleshy leaves, such as cacti and succulents, do not require as much watering as the plants with thinner leaves, because they are able to retain moisture within their tissues. On the other hand, plants with proportionately large leaves require more frequent watering, because they have a larger surface from which the plant loses water vapour. Again, there are generally two distinct periods in the year of the average plant, the season when it is growing fast and another when it is resting. During the first it needs plenty of watering, which should normally tail off until the dormant period is reached. During the resting period the amount of water given should be quite small. Another important factor is the conditions under which a house plant is living. When the temperature is high and the light is bright, its demand for water is high. A plant kept continuously in a cool place requires much less frequent watering.

Also a plant habitually needs more frequent watering if it is in a well-drained pot. If it is in a clay pot, from which the rate of evaporation is higher, it needs more watering than it would if planted in a plastic one.

Plants in small pots and those that are becoming pot-bound also need more watering. On the other hand, newly re-potted plants and those in large pots should be treated more cautiously.

Generally it is better to under-water *slightly* rather than to give excess, to allow the soil, which is darker in colour when it is moist, to dry out to a considerable extent before watering is repeated. Give plenty of water during the spring and summer, when the plants are growing and little when they are resting. It is best to use water with the chill off and a few plants prefer rainwater or softened water.

Each watering must be thorough with a fairly long interval between; a daily dribble is valueless. Because of the possibility of chilling when the temperature falls at night, house plants should be watered in the morning during the winter. In summer they should not be watered in direct sunshine as any water falling on the leaves is likely to scorch them.

There are two principal ways of watering — by plunging the pots, or by watering from above. A plunged pot should be stood in water up to half its depth and allowed to stay there until the soil is fairly moist but not waterlogged. The water will be absorbed by capillary action. After this, the pot should be drained and put back in its place. When watering from above it is important to have a space of at least 2·5 cm (1 in) between the rim and the level of the soil. Use a small watering can with a long, narrow spout which can be inserted between the leaves so that they do not get wetted. It is important to remember, however, that some plants, such as cyclamen and saintpaulias, can be seriously damaged by having their leaves, stalks, and

growing centres splashed, and these must be watered from below. Unless they are aquatic plants, such as *Cyperus diffusus*, or great moisture lovers such as *Helxine soleirolii* (Mind Your Own Business), house plants should never stand permanently in water in a saucer.

Packing wet peat around pots and standing them in pebble trays has already been discussed, and these methods can help where the demand for water is very high, or if watering can only be carried out infrequently, or when the plants have to be left unattended for a few days. There are also automatic self-watering and wick-watering pots on the market that are useful for emergencies, but none of these devices is a real substitute for personal attention. There are also inexpensive instruments available for indicating when water is necessary, but their use must be tempered with experience.

Plants in the Bathroom and Kitchen
Besides being an ideal home for new plants of a delicate nature, and a convalescent home for flagging plants, the bathroom with its warm and moist conditions is far and away the best permanent home for many of the more temperamental plants. In this respect almost all the plants in the vast aroid family would be suitable and some of the exotic ferns from tropical forests, although care would have to be exercised when selecting plants to ensure that aroids with potential growth suited to the size of the bathroom are chosen. The king of philodendrons, *P. eichleri*, produces its large leaves from a stout central stem and develops into a plant some 3 m (10 ft) in height, with a spread of leaves taking in an area of similar diameter. With such a plant most bathrooms would be filled to capacity, and this is not quite what you are looking for when considering the possibility of using plants to enhance the beauty of the homestead! Fortunately the foregoing plant is one of the exceptions.

There are a great many others of more modest dimension that are among the finest of indoor plants. And what better choice could there be than the Sweetheart Plant, *Philodendron scandens*, with its glossy green leaves. This plant, like the scindapsus and other aroids with smaller leaves, can be adapted either to climb or trail, depending on what is required.

With aroids you need not be restricted to purely foliage plants as the anthuriums with their long-lasting spathe flowers, mostly in

11

shades of red, will give a fine display and need only a warm, moist and shaded situation to succeed. Where space is limited the best choice will be *A. scherzerianum* (Flaming Sword). Also with spathe flowers there is *Spathiphyllum wallisii* (Sail Plant), the white sail-like spathes of which are produced almost throughout the year, and will surely be more numerous if the plants are grown in the steamy warmth of the bathroom.

If you are fortunate enough to have a say in the design of your house, persuade the architect to allow for recessed shelfing in the bathroom. This is an excellent solution to finding shelf space for plants.

The only limiting factor concerning which plants can and cannot be used is the size of the bathroom, as almost all the foliage plants needing warm conditions will be suitable. However, there is one very important precaution that you should take, and that is to ensure that all plants

are kept well out of harm's way when aerosol sprays are being used, unless these are specifically intended for treating plants. Also, with the clouds of talcum powder that are usually prevalent in the bathroom it is necessary to clean the foliage of bathroom plants more frequently than those in other rooms. In most instances this can be done by placing the plant in the bathtub and spraying it over. The extra moisture will usually be to the benefit of the plant.

The kitchen windowsill is also an ideal spot for many plants, particularly spring-flowering subjects, which seem to favour this location. The often problematical saintpaulias and pelargoniums also tend to do well.

The fact that the kitchen has few, if any, heavy curtaining around its windows plays an important part in getting the best out of your plants. And, provided water is kept off leaves and flowers, the majority of our indoor plants will tolerate much more direct sunlight than

BELOW:
Houseplants often welcome a summer vacation on the patio, where a riot of colour and textures can be created — a previously dull and uninteresting corner can be transformed into an exotic and idyllic haven.

one might expect. However, it may be better to remove plants that are likely to be harmed from the windowsill during the hottest part of the day.

To make the movement of plants a less tedious business it will help if they are all grown in a container of some kind so that the complete collection of plants may be transferred at one go. Windowsill troughs are neat, and plants almost invariably do better when they are grouped together than when they are dotted about a room.

Troughs for plants can be utilized in several different ways, and there is no reason why they should not simply be put to use as pot holders with a selection of plants placed in them. An improvement on this is to place a 5 cm (2 in) layer of gravel in the bottom of the container before setting in the plant pots. Thereafter the gravel should be kept moist, but the plant pots must at no time be allowed actually to stand in water. An alternative to gravel would be to fill the trough with moist peat, packing it up to the rims of the pots in which the plants are growing. Both methods will help to maintain a reasonable level of humidity around the plants, which is one of the most important requirements of all plants that are growing in a relatively dry atmosphere. Leaves should be sponged frequently to remove any grease.

By leaving plants in their individual pots they may all be attended to as individuals when it comes to watering and feeding. However, if plants that are reasonably compatible in their watering and feeding needs are grouped together there is no reason why they should not be removed from their pots and planted individually in the trough. When planting in this way a soil containing a reasonably high proportion of peat should be used. Following planting, water must be given sparingly until plants are obviously established in the new medium, and at no time should water be given excessively as few of the troughs will have holes from which

excess moisture may easily and quickly drain.

The average-size kitchen is seldom suited to the growing of larger plants, yet there is often the need for using plants to divide the working part of the kitchen from the small dining recess that is part of the kitchen area. Although there may be little chance of using large plants there is ample scope for using smaller plants placed on tiered shelving. In this respect, smaller plants in decorative pots placed among other small ornaments can be most effective, and the entire scene will be enhanced if some of the plants trail over the edges of the shelves.

Most of the plant pot holders offered for sale are more costly than the plants that are placed in them, but there are also the more reasonable plastic items. Some are attractive while others are not so appealing to the eye. For narrow kitchen shelves, however, there are some excellent plastic plant trays that are shallow enough not to be obtrusive.

Choosing and caring for healthy plants

There are many factors which will determine the plants you choose to buy for your home, the most important of which — if the plants are to thrive — is the environment which you are able to provide. As discussed in the previous chapter, light, temperature and humidity are all important. In addition you will have to decide how much attention you are prepared to devote to the plants, and select accordingly those which need a lot of tender loving care and those hardier specimens which can tolerate occasional periods of neglect. To help you with the choice, all the plants in the alphabetical sections of the following chapters are rated for ease of care with stars. One star is an easy plant that is very tolerant, two stars indicate a plant that is more difficult to grow successfully but which should thrive with attention. Three stars indicate a difficult plant to grow in the home and one best avoided by beginners. However, there will be many gardeners who like the challenge of a more difficult plant.

The pleasure lies in choosing plants because you like the look of them — whether you are drawn to classically shaped green foliage plants, or find the luscious blooms of the flowering varieties more appealing. In the latter event, you will be able to choose plants to suit every season of the year, so that it will truly seem as if you have brought a flourishing garden indoors.

When buying houseplants, don't be tempted to save a few pence by taking a tired-looking specimen in the hope that you will magically be able to revive it. The chances are that it had a bad start in life that will permanently affect its health and therefore its appearance; far better to go for the sturdy good-looking plant that, with wise care, will beautify your home for many months and possibly provide more plants from cuttings.

When you buy a plant, make sure that it isn't wilting, that its leaves are not damaged, turning yellow, or brown, or about to fall off, and that its roots are not coming out of the bottom of the pot. Choose a flowering plant that is mostly in bud, with only a few flowers out, and have a particularly good look to make sure there are no pests like greenfly, scale or mealy-bug on the leaves or stems. Plants are not cheap nowadays, and you would not buy a damaged product, so why buy an ailing plant?

When you are bringing it home, the nursery or shop should have wrapped it up well but, if not, try to provide some cover for the whole plant to protect it against cold and draughts. The changes in environment since it left its home nursery will have been considerable, and it is important to minimize these as much as possible, and to fuss over it a bit for the first few days while it settles down.

It may need watering at once; if the pot feels light and the compost is dry on the surface, try immersing the whole container in tepid water. If air bubbles come up through the water, the plant has been allowed to get very dry, and it is best left in the water until no more air bubbles appear. Then it can be taken out, the surplus water allowed to drain through the drainage holes, and put in its permanent position, on an ordinary saucer or pot saucer to prevent the damp damaging your furniture. The tables on the following pages will help you to choose the plant or group of plants most likely to live happily in particular conditions. Outlined below are the most important aspects of care which will keep plants looking good for as long as possible.

Cleaning and Polishing Leaves

Plants grown indoors do not have their leaves washed regularly by the rain like their outdoor counterparts, and as the leaves play such an important role in maintaining health, it is necessary to see that their pores are kept free from dust and smoke grime, and that a film does not form on their surfaces which will reduce the amount of light reaching them. Although perhaps nowadays, with centrally-heated rooms and electric fires, this is not such a major problem, it is still necessary to keep the foliage clean and, of course, it improves the plant's appearance.

Both the upper and lower surfaces of the leaves should be sponged with tepid water and if they are very dirty, soapy water can be used, but it must be thoroughly rinsed off afterwards. Plants with finely cut and delicate foliage must be cleansed by thorough spraying. Some people like to give them a good shine, but olive oil, which does achieve this end quite effectively, tends to attract dust, especially in the pores where it is easily lodged. There are, however, proprietary leaf cleaners that appear to be quite safe and give a shine lasting for months.

FAR LEFT:
Modern conservatories, made of aluminium, enable an abundance of light to reach the plants. Plants such as dieffenbachias, pileas, codiaeums, dracaenas and ficus will then grow to perfection, forming a screen of colourful leaves.

BELOW:
Dracaena fragrans is one of the larger members of the family, having broad strap-like leaves, with a golden band down their centres. It is a plant that will tolerate indirect sunlight.

Plants for particular conditions
bushy foliage plants

Condition	Acorus gramineus 'Variegatus' (Grass)	Aglaonemas	Araucaria excelsa	Aspidistra elatior (A. lurida)	Aucuba japonica 'Variegata'	Begonia maculata	B. masoniana	B. rex	Bromeliads (cryptanthus and nidulariums)	Calathea mackoyana	Cordyline (Dracaena) terminalis	Cyperus diffusus (Grass)	Dieffenbachias	Dizygotheca (Aralia) elegantissima	Dracaenas	D. sanderiana	D. deremensis 'Bausei'	D. fragrans
Easy to grow									■			■						
For average rooms with reasonable lighting, some sunshine, and which are maintained heated for some hours daily during the winter			■								■	■						
Unheated areas (halls, landings and staircases)	■		■	■	■							■						
For centrally-heated rooms. (The air surrounding the plants should be humid.)		■	■			■	■	■	■	■	■		■	■	■	■	■	■
Rooms without sun	■	■	■			■		■	■	■	■	■			■	■	■	■
Plants that flourish in full sun																		
Suitable for dark rooms and full shade			■	■														
Small plants suitable for limited areas	■								■							■		
Large plants suitable for offices and large spaces						■					■		■	■	■			
Plants for flower arrangers	■		■			■		■						■				
Plants that withstand fumes, e.g. gas, cooking, tobacco, etc.			■	■														

16

	Fatshedera lizei	Fatsia japonica	Ficus	F. lyrata	Fittonias	Grevillea robusta	Helxine soleirolii	Marantas	Monstera deliciosa 'Borsigiana'	Pandanus veitchii	Peperomias	Philodendrons	P. erubescens	Pileas	Saxifraga stolonifera	Schefflera actinophylla	Setcreasea purpurea	Tolmiea menziesii
Easy to grow	■	■				■	■	■							■		■	■
For average rooms with reasonable lighting, some sunshine, and which are maintained heated for some hours daily during the winter	■	■	■			■	■		■		■		■		■	■	■	■
Unheated areas (halls, landings and staircases)	■	■				■	■									■		■
For centrally-heated rooms. (The air surrounding the plants should be humid.)	■		■		■			■	■	■	■		■	■	■		■	
Rooms without sun	■	■					■	■			■					■		■
Plants that flourish in full sun																		
Suitable for dark rooms and full shade			■			■	■		■		■			■				
Small plants suitable for limited areas					■			■		■	■			■	■			■
Large plants suitable for offices and large spaces		■	■	■		■			■			■	■					
Plants for flower arrangers		■									■						■	
Plants that withstand fumes, e.g. gas, cooking, tobacco, etc.	■	■				■			■			■			■	■		

climbing and trailing foliage plants

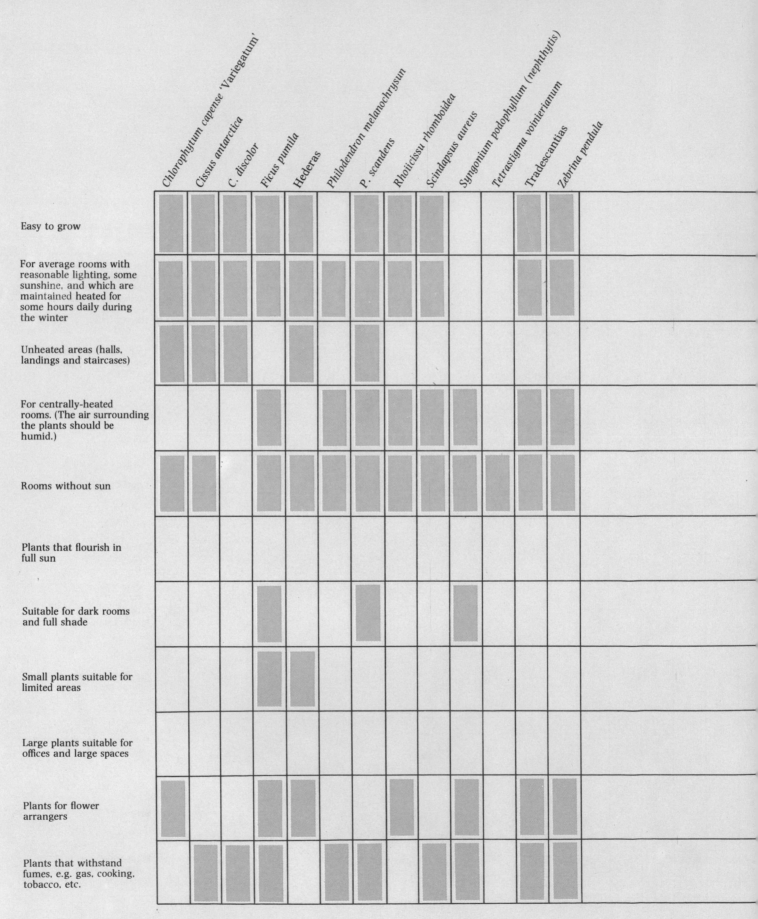

flowering plants

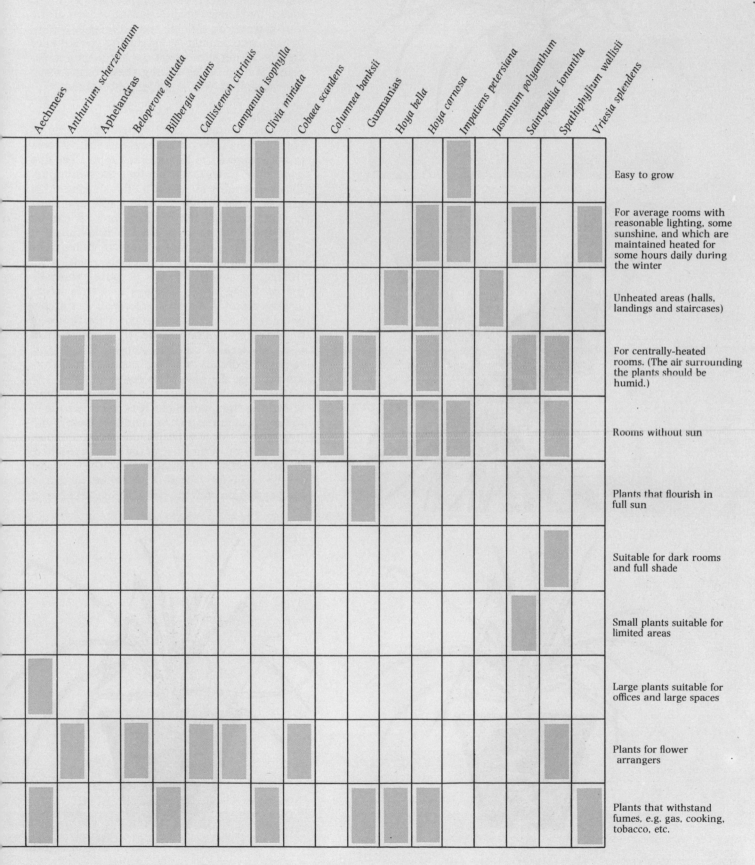

Feeding

There are no differences in the nutritional requirements of houseplants from those of the multitude that grow in the open. When plants are first purchased the compost usually contains enough fertilizer to last for some months, but thereafter they benefit from small regular feeds (there are several proprietary solutions especially blended for houseplants) given at the time of watering. Foliage and summer-flowering house plants should be fed during the summer and the winter-flowering ones in the winter. No plants should be fed during their resting time, otherwise they will be undesirably forced.

Repotting

This is an operation to be postponed as long as possible because most houseplants flourish best in what appears to be too small a pot. The day does come, however, when they are pot-bound. This is normally indicated by the slowing up of growth, rapid drying out of the soil, and roots growing through the drainage hole. It can be confirmed by knocking out the root-ball. If it consists mainly of a matted mass of visible roots and little soil, then the plant needs repotting.

The pot chosen for this purpose should be the next size larger, perhaps two sizes larger in the case of a vigorous grower. If it is a clay pot, a layer of crocks should cover the drainage hole. This should be followed by a thin layer of peat, followed by potting compost. The plant is removed from its old pot, the old crocks removed from the base of its root-ball and a few of the matted outside roots loosened without disturbing the main roots. It is placed on top of the compost in the new pot and the space round it gradually filled with slightly moist compost until the level of the base of the stem is reached, firming gently. The final level of the compost should be about 2·5 cm (1 in) below the rim of the pot. Finally, tap the pot down several times,

then water and place in a shady place for a week, spraying daily. After this, the plant can be put back in its usual quarters.

A good compost for this purpose is a mixture of two parts commercial potting compost and one part peat. In addition, there are nowadays several proprietary loamless composts that are very good for many plants.

In the case of very large houseplants re-potting is difficult to do safely. The difficulty can be overcome by topdressing, which is usually done in the spring. The top 2·5–5 cm (1–2 in) of soil is carefully removed from the pot, and replaced with fresh compost.

Shaping and Resting

The smaller, softer, quickly growing plants such as Busy Lizzie and the Aluminium Plant (*Pilea cadierei*) can be made more bushy by 'pinching'. This means nipping out the tip of a shoot when the plant is growing well, removing the stem with the first pair, and sometimes the second pair, of leaves from the tip, and making the cut or break just above the next lowest pair, so that no stub is left on the plant. New shoots will then grow lower down from between the stem and the point where a leaf joins the stem, but the tip of the shoot will not grow any more. 'Pinching' can be done two or three times at about monthly intervals in spring and early summer.

'Resting' plants is very important; it is usually needed after flowering, though some plants have a slightly different life cycle and go on growing after this for a while. To rest a plant, gradually give it less water, and put it in a lower temperature than when it is growing. Sometimes the shoots need to be cut right back. The plant becomes almost dormant and may remain like that for several months; its rest period may be in summer or winter, depending on the flowering time which will vary according to which part of the world it comes from.

ABOVE:
Busy Lizzies are easily-grown plants which can be formed into a busy shape by pinching out the growing tips of the shoots. Nip the shoots back to a position close to where a pair of leaves join the stem. New shoots will develop from the axils of the leaves

LEFT:
From time to time it is necessary to repot plants into larger containers. Repot houseplants as soon as they start into active growth (1), which is usually during the spring. Turn the plant upside down, support the soil-ball with your hand and knock the edge of the pot on a firm surface. The pot will come away from the soil-ball (2), which if necessary can be trimmed and then set into a pot partly filled with fresh compost (3). Trickle soil around the root-ball, firming it well . (4). Replace the label and give the plant a good watering (5).

Holiday Care

Houseplants, like pets, must be considered at holiday time. Most people do not really want to bother their neighbours at such times, and if the plants are thoroughly watered beforehand, they can usually be left in a cool place quite satisfactorily for the duration of a *short* holiday. If the holiday is rather more prolonged, the pots can be surrounded with moist peat, or stood on a water-filled pebble tray. For such periods automatic watering equipment is useful.

If the weather is warm, after watering each plant can be placed, pot first, into a polythene bag of suitable size and the top open edges closed by twisting together and binding them with tape. This will conserve moisture. But be sure the bag is not touching any leaves.

When Things go Wrong

You may find that, in spite of all your care, your plants are not thriving as they should. Usually this means that either what is your idea of a little water is the plant's idea of too much, or your views on the amount of warmth required do not coincide. In practically every case of poor plant growth, the remedy is to alter your care and management of it, to give less or more water, less or more humidity, change the temperature or the light, repot, and so on. Weak plants, or plants which are having to contend with the wrong environment, are the ones which will be infected by insect pests. Healthy plants are usually not attacked.

If your plants do succumb to pests or diseases, a later chapter tells you how to cope.

RIGHT:
The Fiddle-back Fig. known botanically as Ficus lyrata (F. pandurata), *is a very distinctive member of the fig family. Eventually it forms a tall, handsome and weeping tree, with attractively shaped large and shiny medium-green leaves marked with cream-coloured veins.*

FAR RIGHT:
Colourful urns and containers can be made even more attractive by placing plants in them, such as Chlorophytum comosum 'Variegatum' and Cissus antarctica. Allow the plants to trail over the sides of the pot so that the foliage blends with the container.

Foliage plants

Although flowering houseplants are often very spectacular and beautiful, foliage plants should always play an important part in any collection in the home. Many will flourish in lighting conditions that most flowering plants would not tolerate. And of course they are usually attractive for a much longer period.

Foliage plants are available in a surprisingly wide range of forms and habits – from the low golden hummocks of *Helxine solierolii aurea* (Mind Your Own Business), that will tumble over the edge of a pot, to the large rubber plants and philodendrons that will reach the ceiling of a modern house in a surprisingly short time.

Once a few foliage plants have been collected, the sheer variety of leaf shapes, colours and markings starts to become apparent. Many leaves are as colourful as most flowers. The well-known coleus, which is one of the few foliage plants that can be raised quickly and easily from seed, demonstrates both the range of vivid colours and the wonderful variegations that can be found in leaves. There's nothing drab about a good croton (*Codiaeum variegatum*), with its brilliant red, orange or yellow leaves enhanced by striking variegations, nor can *Setcreasea purpurea* be overlooked with its strap-like foliage in attractive shades of purple. *Gynura aurantiaca* is another purple plant, only this time it is the hairs that provide the rich colour on the leaves, giving it the velvet-like appearance which led to its descriptive common name the Velvet Nettle.

in their variegations or interesting leaf shapes. Marantas, pileas and fittonias are examples of plants that provide year-round interest with variegation alone, and there is a whole range of plants with plain green leaves that are grown for their interesting shapes. The Swiss Cheese Plant (*Monstera deliciosa*) is popular for its deeply cut foliage, and philodendrons have the merit not only of leaves that are attractively shaped, but that are positioned in such a way that they give the whole plant a distinctive shape.

There are even foliage plants that will amuse – marantas (Prayer Plants) obediently fold their leaves as if in prayer when the lights go out; the Sensitive Plant, *Mimosa pudica*, will sulkily fold up its leaflets and tuck the whole leaf away if anyone touches it; and for those that like the more gruesome, there are plants like the Venus's Flytraps which will devour the odd fly or two.

Other foliage plants are grown for their constant desire to produce new offspring in unconventional ways. The well-known *Chlorophytum comosum* produces replicas of itself on the ends of long stalks, while bryophyllums sprout tiny plantlets along the edges of their leaves.

The positioning of foliage plants is a matter of choice, but those with brightly coloured or variegated leaves are usually best given good light, as this will tend to strengthen the colours. They will be quite happy on a north-facing windowsill. Plants with green leaves, on the other hand, are usually better kept in a shady position, where their leaves will be a deeper green.

Generally, foliage plants will appreciate a feed with a high nitrogen fertilizer. Those with glossy leaves will also benefit from an occasional wipe over with tepid water, and you can lightly brush dust off those with hairy leaves.

There is a word of warning for pet owners. A few plants, such as dieffenbachias and philodendrons, are poisonous. If the leaves of some dieffenbachia species are eaten, there could be fatal consequences. And obviously this warning should also be heeded if there are babies and children in the home. Always wash your hands thoroughly after handling a dieffenbachia.

Aglaonema**

16°C (61°F). South East Asia.

These are foliage houseplants, and have large leaves, variegated in some way. They are members of the aroid plant family, the Araceae, which contains such plants as the philodendrons and dieffenbachias, and come from all over south-east Asia, so they need quite warm temperatures and high humidity.

Aglaonemas grow upright, fairly tall, and the·leaves can be 23 cm (9 in) or more in length, and about 8–10 cm (3–4 in) wide, depending on the species. There is a very attractive one which is usually sold under the name *A. pseudobracteatum*, though it is probably a variety of *A. commutatum*. The leaves have a large central area of yellow. *A. costatum* has dark green leaves spotted white, and a bright white midrib, and *A. commutatum* has diagonal creamy lines running parallel to the side veins.

Aglaonemas need a fairly high temperature and humidity, especially in winter, with a minimum of 10°C (50°F) and no draughts. A good light, or even some shade, is suitable, though the variegation will be better in the light. Water and feed normally, resting in winter, and do not subject to gas or paraffin fumes.

New plants can be raised from cuttings or by dividing mature clumps. When propagating, warm, moist and shaded corditions are essential. Fresh sphagnum peat will be the best medium to start plants off in.

Araucaria heterophylla (syn. *A excelsa*)*

Norfolk Island Pine 7°C (45°F). Norfolk Island. Typical needle pine leaves are shaded dark and light green and develop on horizontal branches that radiate from the main stem. The spaced tiers of leaves are the principal attraction of this plant which is one of the true aristocrats among the foliage plants that are suited to cooler room conditions. Set in a well-lit airy position, watering freely in spring and summer, less in winter.

When potting, clay pots will help to balance plants better than plastic ones as plants are inclined to be top heavy. Although plant growth will be slower in loam-based mixture, a better plant will result than if the plant is grown in a peat medium. Clay pots must have a good layer of broken pots placed in the bottom before soil is introduced, as good drainage is most important.

New plants may be raised from cuttings of stem tips, or from seed – the latter method produces plants with more attractive symmetrical growth. However, seed is very difficult to obtain, so it is often better to seek out young plants that may be grown on.

Asparagus*

7°C (45°F). South Africa.

A. asparagoides (*A. medioloides*) (Smilax) and *A. setaceus* (*A. plumosus*) (Asparagus Fern) make very effective potted plants, or plants for the wall of the heated conservatory, but are most frequently seen as cut foliage in floral arrangements and other designs created by the florist.

One of the most durable of potted ornamental asparagus, and the one most frequently seen, is *A. densiflorus* (*A. sprengeri*), which can either be grown as a trailing plant or encouraged to climb a plant frame. Choose a loam-based soil and a well-lit spot, shaded from direct sun. Feed every two weeks and give plenty of water in spring and summer. Keep just moist in winter.

New plants may be raised from seed sown in a temperature of around 20°C (70°F) in the spring, but it will be much simpler to propagate by division of roots in the spring.

LEFT:
Aglaonema commutatum is a member of the aroid plant family, displaying leaves with attractive blotching. Aglaonemas require both a fairly high temperature and humidity, and a minimum temperature of 10°C (50°F). They do not like to be placed in a draught.

25

Aspidistra elatior (syn. *A. lurida*)*

Cast Iron Plant 7°C (45°F). China.

The great favourite of the Victorian era, the aspidistra still has much to commend it and is most effective when seen in its traditional setting, atop a Victorian plant pedestal and growing in a rather grand and flowery Victorian plant pot.

The oblong-lanceolate leaves, up to 50 cm (20 in) long, are green and somewhat coarse in appearance and are produced on short stalks that emerge directly from the soil. There is a rare variegated form with creamy-white striped leaves, but this needs reasonable light to maintain the colouring.

As its common name suggests, this plant is among the hardiest of all foliage houseplants, withstanding with equanimity gas, deep shade, neglect, heat, dust, dryness of air and soil, but not bright sunshine. Any care, however, brings its rewards. All it asks for is to be kept moist, given moderate humidity and reasonable warmth. It likes having its leaves sponged occasionally and to be given spells out of doors in the summer rain. The leaves of both the dark-green and variegated varieties are prized by flower arrangers.

Propagate at almost any time by diving older clumps and potting them in a rich loam-based mixture.

and reasonably light conditions are needed, but strong sunlight must be avoided. A peaty soil is essential and it should be kept moist, but never soggy wet.

Raise new *B. rex* plants by slitting the veins on the undersides of a mature leaf in places before placing it on a mixture of peat and sand. It may be necessary to peg the leaves down with hairpin-shaped wires, or by placing small pebbles on top of the leaf. Alternatively, the stronger and older leaves may be cut up into 2·5 cm (1 in) squares and simply placed on moist peat and sand. This is a fascinating means of propagation, but it is extremely important that the propagating medium must at no time dry out as the small leaf sections will quickly shrivel up and die. Moistness of a happy medium should be the aim, as leaf sections will also rot readily in very wet conditions.

Another beautiful begonia is *B. masoniana*, with its remarkably patterned leaves rather than gorgeously coloured foliage. The noticeably bright green leaves, with pointed tips, have superimposed a distinctive, curious purplish-black cross reminiscent of the German award. So close is the resemblance that this species has become known as the 'Iron Cross' begonia. It is slower growing than *Begonia rex*, but its cultivation is much the same. Contributing to its beauty, it has fleshy, red-pink stems, which contrast magnificently with the brilliant green foliage. It is one of the finest of the begonias.

Begonia*/**

15°C (60°F). South East Asia.

The king of the begonias, grown entirely for its colourful foliage, is *Begonia rex*. Blended into or overlaid on the green wrinkled leaves can be found a kaleidoscope of colours — red, pink, silver, cream, grey, lavender and maroon.

Although plants may be encouraged to grow to 60 cm (2 ft) in height and 60 cm (2 ft) in diameter in ideal conditions in the greenhouse, they are usually seen as much smaller plants decorating windowsills and in mixed arrangements with other plants. It should be grown in semi-shade, out of reach of gas fumes and kept in an outer container filled with moist peat. Mildew on leaves, which appears as white circular spots, is one of the most troublesome problems and is most prevalent in surroundings that are dank and airless. So a buoyant humid atmosphere

Calathea***

Peacock Plant 13–16°C (55–61°F). Brazil.

Exotically-patterned leaves in many shades of green and brown are the order of the day here, and *C. makoyana* with its exquisitely patterned leaves is one of the most striking of foliage plants. It fully justifies its common name of Peacock Plant. The leaves of *C. zebrina* are light and dark green and have a texture that is reminiscent of velvet. *C. insignis* has narrower

more densely clustered foliage that is also very impressive.

Calatheas are not plants for the beginner; the suggested minimum temperature must be maintained, and the general conditions surrounding the plants should be moist and shaded. Ideally they should be watered and sprayed with rainwater as tap water may leave white marks on the foliage.

Propagate calatheas by division of the rhizomes in summer, and at all stages of growth use a peaty, open soil.

Chlorophytum*
Spider Plant 7°C (45°F). South Africa.

This very graceful green and cream striped grass-like foliage plant can be seen on the windowsill of almost all who keep plants indoors. The two varieties most readily available are *C. comosum* 'Variegatum' with leaves up to 30–45 cm (12–18 in) long, and *C. elatum*, whose leaves grow up to 60 cm (24 in).

Chlorophytums need little more than a light windowsill position, ample watering in spring and summer, and feeding with a liquid manure once a week in the summer. These accommodating plants are also very effective for hanging baskets.

Excessive watering in winter when temperatures indoors are generally lower will cause brown streaks to appear in the centre of some leaves.

It is advisable to pot chlorophytums on into larger containers annually in March or April using a loam-based compost.

Propagation is simplicity itself. Plants soon produce long arching stems which bear inconspicuous whitish flowers and tiny plantlets which root extremely readily. Just peg them down into a pot of compost until they root.

Cissus antarctica*

Kangaroo Vine 10°C (50°F). Australia.

This is a very easy-to-grow, tough, fast-growing, self-clinging climber, reaching, if permitted, a height of 2·5 m (8 ft). It is excellent grown as a room divider. It has lovely, fresh green oval leaves, which are well veined.

Although it does best in good light, out of strong sun, it may also do fairly well in sunless and more shady rooms. It is quite tolerant of lower temperatures. It enjoys a medium humid atmosphere, and should be well watered at intervals during the summer. Between waterings the compost should be allowed to dry out almost completely. It needs very little water during the winter.

The Kangaroo Vine is easily propagated by layering or taking a cutting with a single leaf.

Codiaeum (Croton)***

Joseph's Coat 16—18°C (61—64°F). South East Asia.

Codiaeums are magnificent evergreen plants that are available in many shades of orange, red and yellow, white, cream and purple-black, with some plants having all these colours in many shades present in a single leaf.

In keeping with the majority of plants with highly-coloured leaves, Joseph's Coat is not at all easy to care for and will require the conditions that most tender plants demand and the skills of the experienced grower to maintain them in good order. In ideal greenhouse conditions plants will attain a height of 3 m (10 ft) or more, by which time they are a truly magnificent sight; as a pot plant the usual height is 60 cm (2 ft). Maximum sunlight, though no scorching, is essential if they are to retain their exotic colouring, and it is also important that the soil should at no time be allowed to dry out. Liquid feeding of established plants once a week during summer must not be neglected, and it will be found that mature plants will require fertilizer at least double the strength that the manufacturer recommends. When potting these plants, it is advisable to use a loam-based compost or a proprietary peat mix.

Although conditions are not ideal, crotons will go on for a considerable time in a warm room that is well provided with windows, but draughts and sudden drops in temperature can prove fatal.

Propagate by means of cuttings about 13 cm (5 in) in length taken from the top-most growth of the plant. Treat the severed end with rooting powder before inserting the cutting in a peat and sand mixture. The temperature in the propagator must be in the region of 20°C (70°F).

RIGHT: Cissus antarctica, *the Kangaroo Vine, does well in most places. It is a natural climber, bearing attractive shiny green leaves. New plants can be formed by rooting leaf cuttings in a sandy soil.*

FAR RIGHT: *The richly coloured leaves of* Codiaeum variegatum pictum *are a delight to see — they are often brighter than the flowers of many other plants.*

28

Coleus*

Flame Nettle 13°C (55°F) South East Asia.

Of the less expensive foliage houseplants there is none that can compare with the Flame Nettle when it comes to leaf colouring. From a single packet of seed sown in the greenhouse in the spring come plants with colours and colour combinations of an almost infinite variety, including purple, red, bronze, yellow and white. Although seed-grown plants are not as good as named varieties that have been raised from cuttings (taken at any time when they are available provided there is a warm greenhouse or propagating case available for starting them off in) you can, nevertheless, get some very fine plants if the best colours are selected for growing on in larger pots.

Pinch out the growing points regularly to promote bushy side growth. Coleus are generally greedy in respect of feeding, but need for feeding can be reduced by potting plants on into large pots – it would be quite possible to have spring sown seedlings growing in 18 cm (7 in) pots by the autumn. Use a loam-based mixture when potting and be sure to select only the best coloured plants, as there is no point in lavishing extra care on some of the more cabbage-like plants that one may find among almost any batch of seedlings.

All coleus do best in good light and reasonable warmth with a little tender care thrown in for good measure. They may reach 45 cm (18 in) in height. Although seldom grown on for a second year, good forms can be overwintered for cuttings to be taken from them in spring.

Cyperus*

Umbrella Grass 13°C (55°F). Africa.

Never allow plants to remain wet in their pots for long periods, is almost standard advice when the experienced plantsman is asked for his, or her, advice on watering. However, there are a few exceptions to this rule, and the moisture-loving, rush-like cyperus is one of them. The loam mixture must be kept permanently wet, and it is usually advisable to allow the plant pot actually to stand in water (for most pot plants this would almost certainly mean a quick death). Lack of moisture will make the tips of the leaves turn brown, or become infested with red spider mite. Use a good potting compost, and feed during the summer.

Cyperus develop grass-like growth at the top of slender stems which give an umbrella appearance, hence the common name. Stalks of *C. diffusus* are about 60 cm (2 ft) tall and more numerous than those of *C. alternifolius* which attain a height of 1·8−2·4 m (6−8 ft) even when roots are confined to pots.

Dividing mature clumps is the best method of propagation.

Dieffenbachia***

Dumb Cane 15°C (60°F). Tropical America.

There are many exciting plants to be found in this genus of outstanding foliage plants, but only very few are suited to other than warm greenhouse conditions. Warm, moist and shaded conditions suit them best, protected from draughts. Use a rich loam-based compost.

By far the best one for indoor use is *D.*

BELOW:

Coleus plants are among the best known foliage plants. Coleus do have flowers, but they are best picked off as they develop, to direct the plant's energy to producing attractive leaves. These plants are of the Rainbow Strain.

BELOW, RIGHT:

Dieffenbachia picta 'Exotica' is very attractive, with a compact habit and variegated cream, white and green leaves. It is a plant that needs to be kept away from draughts and placed in a warm and shaded spot. Keep the soil moist.

'Exotica', which has a compact habit and superbly variegated cream, white and green leaves. The variety 'Tropic Snow' is an even bolder plant attaining a height of some 1·5 m (5 ft) with larger leaves and darker green colouring – a fine plant if space is not a problem. Another species likely to be encountered is *D. seguina*. As plants age, typical arum inflorescences are produced from the topmost leaf axils, but as these do nothing for the plant they should be removed.

You should always wash your hands after cutting any part of dieffenbachia plants, as the sap contains a poison that could render you speechless if enough of it gets on to your tongue.

Dieffenbachias can be propagated by removing young plants from around the base of the stem of the parent, or the main stem of mature plants can be put into 5 cm (2 in) sections and partly buried in moist peat in a propagating case that is kept at around 20°C (70°F).

Dionaea muscipula**
Venus's Flytrap 13°C (55°F). South Carolina.
These insectivorous plants trap the animal protein that they need, but it is possible to keep thriving plants of this kind by feeding them ordinary mineral or vegetable nitrogen and other nutrients.

The end half of the *Dionaea muscipula* leaf is modified into two pads with teeth on the margins and bristles in the leaf centre. When the central bristles are touched by a fly or other insect the two parts of the leaf fold together so that the teeth interlock and the insect is then trapped inside, to be digested at leisure by the plant. It sounds gruesome, but is a fascinating thing to watch.

It is a small plant no more than 15 cm (6 in) tall when in flower, and consists of a rosette of leaves close to the soil for the rest of the year. The flowers are white and quite pretty, blooming in mid summer.

The compost should be a mixture of peat and living sphagnum moss, which can be bought from garden shops and some florists. Coolness in summer and winter alike will produce a good plant. Repot in the spring.

Dizygotheca elegantissima***
False Aralia 15°C (60°F). New Hebrides.
Formerly included in the genus Aralia, these graceful foliage plants will develop into small trees when cultivated in ideal surroundings. Plants are at their best when about 1·5 m (5 ft) in height, thereafter the leaves begin to lose their fine, rich blue-black filigree appearance, and become much coarser and broader. But this is not likely to affect the grower of indoor plants unless he is particularly skilful in their care.

Moist, lightly shaded and evenly warm conditions are most essential, as is a rich gritty soil and regular watering.

Seed is the best method of raising plants, but it will be difficult to obtain.

Dracaena**
Dragon Plant 13°C (55°F). Tropical Africa.
All dracaenas are very lovely, comparatively tall, slow-growing, foliage plants. Most species have long, firm, silky, long-lasting, pointed leaves, that are variously striped. Most of them shed their lower leaves as they grow taller, but this is not to their disadvantage. While they grow under average conditions, they are at their best in centrally-heated rooms, in which the temperature is never lower than 13°C (55°F) and the humidity is reasonably low. They need to be well watered in the summer, but this must be reduced during winter. Generally dracaenas do well in both bright and medium light, but indirect sunlight is beneficial to the variegated types.

Two more dwarf dracaenas, which are very attractive in the house are *D. godseffiana*, one of the shorter growing types, which has dark-green leaves with pale-yellow spots, and *D. sanderiana*, which is smaller than most, and very attractive with its grey-green leaves bordered with a white band. It thrives in semi-shade, and is a good plant for dish and bottle gardens.

Among the larger types are *D. deremensis* 'Warnecki', which has grey-green leaves with two silver stripes and *D. deremensis* 'Bausei', with its dark-green leaves with a broad central stripe of white, growing from silvery coloured stems. Others are *D. fragrans*, which has broad, strap-shaped leaves with a gold band down their centres, *D. marginata*, which is perhaps a little easier to grow than the rest and has dull red-margined leaves (the variety 'Tricolor' is an excellent recent introduction), and, finally, *D.* 'Firebrand' which is unusual but very lovely, with its narrow pink and red leaves.

ABOVE:
Dracaenas are highly distinctive foliage houseplants, commonly called Dragon Plants. The specimen here is called 'Red Edge'. Dracaenas thrive in a temperature of 13°C (55°F), and can flourish in centrally-heated houses, if provided with adequate humidity.

x Fatshedera lizei*

Ivy Tree 7°C (45°F). Garden Origin.
Attractive five-lobed green leaves are borne on erect stems that become woody with age — provision of a stake to support the plant is essential. There seem to be no limit to the amount of growth that a single stem will put on as you will frequently see them climbing and wandering along staircases and balconies with leading growth tied in to point them in the right direction.

Reasonably easy to care for in cool, lightly shaded conditions, the plant is an interesting man-made cross between *Fatsia* (Aralia) *japonica* and *Hedera helix*, the green ivy. Grow in a rich loam-based mixture, potting on annually in March.

New plants come from taking cuttings in July or August of either the top section of the plant or from single leaves with a piece of stem attached.

Fatsia japonica*

False Castor Oil Plant 2–4°C (36–39°F) Japan.
One of the hardiest of foliage house plants, it will flourish in temperate climates, in shady spots out of doors. As an indoor plant, it grows easily and can become quite large and so is useful in larger spaces. It does not require warmth during winter nor does it need bright light but it should be copiously watered during summer.

The large shiny leaves should be sponged occasionally and the plant will appreciate a day out in the summer rain. A variegated form is obtainable.

New plants are raised from seed sown in spring.

Ficus*/**

7–18°C (45–64°F). Tropical Asia.
The many species in this large genus are very varied and have different cultural requirements. Most frequently seen is the conventional Rubber Plant with its upright habit and glossy green leaves, the care of which may present some problems. The first of the conventional Rubber Plants was *F. elastica*, which gave way to the improved *F. elastica* 'Decora', which in turn has been superseded by the much stronger growing and greatly improved *F. elastica* 'Robusta'. Yet another variety, 'Black Prince', has much darker, almost black leaves.

All of these varieties are tolerant of shady positions, and require a winter night temperature around 16°C (61°F). But, above all, it is most important that water should be given in moderation — the mixture should be well watered and allowed to dry out a little before the next application, as excessive watering will surely damage the root system which will in turn result in loss of leaves. Moderation really is the keyword in most respects and also applies to feeding and potting the plant on into larger containers — the new pot should only be slightly larger than the old one and the need for potting on should only arise every second year unless plants are growing very vigorously.

To improve the appearance of Rubber Plants they should have their leaves cleaned with a soft, damp cloth occasionally.

Most of the other ficus that one is likely to come across — *F. pumila, F. benjamina, F. lyrata, F. diversifolia* and *F. radicans* 'Variegata' — will all need to be kept a little moister, more shaded and some degrees cooler in winter in order to get best results from them.

Ficus pumila is commonly named Creeping Fig on account of its prostrate habit and has small green oval-shaped leaves on thin, wiry, trailing stems. *F. radicans* 'Variegata' is similar in habit with slightly more pointed leaves that are attractively white and green variegated.

If a graceful indoor tree is required then *F. benjamina*, the Weeping Fig, with its glossy green leaves would be an admirable choice. Also developing to tree size in time, *F. lyrata*, the Fiddleback Fig, has glossy leaves that are roughly similar to the body of a violin. It is, however, one of the more difficult of the ficus tribe to care for. *F. diversifolia* is slower growing and takes many years to grow into a smallish bush – the most interesting feature of this plant is the way in which it seems to be constantly producing small berries that appear on even the smallest of plants.

Some of the ficus may be raised from seed, but most of them are propagated from cuttings. Air layering is sometimes used for the Rubber Plant.

Fittonia*
Snakeskin Plant 16°C (61°F). Peru.
Both *Fittonia verschaffeltii* with its red-veined oval leaves and creeping habit, and *F. argyroneura* with ivory-veined leaves of similar shape are difficult plants to care for regardless of the location. They must have constant warmth, fairly heavy shade and high humidity if they are to do well. However, in recent years a miniature form of the latter has appeared on the scene and is proving to be one of the most popular plant introductions. The leaves are small, congested and silvery and the plant has proved to be reasonably easy to care for, certainly much less of a problem than the parent from which it would seem to have sprung. It abhors direct sunlight and cold conditions.

The simplest method of propagation is to place a small plant in the centre of a pot of moist peat and to allow the plant to grow over the peat and root into the medium. When rooted the pieces can be snipped off and potted up individually.

BELOW:
Fittonia argyroneura, *with ivory-veined leaves is particularly distinctive and eye-catching. To be successful it needs constant warmth, shade, and high humidity. It is a plant that tends to trail and ramble.*

Hedera*

Ivy. Frost-free. Europe and Canary Islands.
The ivies are among the easiest of plants to care for given the right treatment and conditions, but they can be something of a problem if conditions are excessively hot or wet. Hot and dry conditions can present a big problem in that plants will be very much more susceptible to attack from red spider mites, and these can reduce ivies to a dry and shrivelled mess in a very short space of time.

There are many varieties to choose from, all of which will put up with cool and lightly shaded spots. *H. canariensis* 'Variegata', with its white and green variegation, the mottle-leaved 'Maculata' and 'Gold Leaf', which has large green leaves with pale yellow centres.

Being natural trailing plants, the smaller-leaved *H. helix* are always much in demand for use in mixed arrangements. There are any number of ivies with green leaves, many of them very similar, but others are very distinct in their appearance, quite a few being cristated. Among the variegated small-leaved ones there are many real gems. 'Little Diamond' and 'Adam', both with grey and white variegated leaves, are two of the best, but there are many more that one may chance to find in shop, garden centre or nursery.

All ivies root readily in a peaty mixture, and best results will be obtained if several cuttings rather than one are put in each pot. Cuttings of smaller-leaved types should be about 8 cm (3 in) in length, while large-leaved ones will require a piece of stem with two leaves attached.

Helxine*

Mind Your Own Business or Baby's Tears 7°C (45°F). Corsica.
Everyone's plant, grows like the proverbial weed (which it is in outdoor situations) and forms neat mounds of minute green leaves. Enjoys all conditions other than those that are badly lit or are excessively hot. Keep moist and make new plants periodically. Dispose of old ones — minute pieces root like weeds.

Maranta***

Prayer Plant 15°C (60°F). Tropical America.
Mostly superb foliage plants, the marantas need warm, moist and shaded locations. An interesting feature of this plant is the way in which leaves fold together as darkness descends. The most striking in this respect is *M. leuconeura* 'Kerchoveana' the leaves of which stand perfectly erect at nightfall — a greenhouse full of them can be an eerie sight when the lights are turned on during the night. This plant has pale grey-green leaves with distinctive dark blotches that make the plant very interesting.

When potting, all the marantas will require a peaty soil, also shallow pots which will be more in proportion with their squat appearance. They will also do better if plant pots can be plunged to their rims in moist peat. Marantas are rapid growers and need potting on several times until they are in final 15 cm (6 in) pots.

A more recent introduction is *M. leuconeura* 'Erythrophylla' which has reddish-brown colouring and intricately marked leaves in a herringbone pattern, and is an altogether bolder grower than the first mentioned. Despite the exotic colouring that would seem to suggest a delicate plant only suitable for the heated greenhouse, it is much more tolerant of room conditions than would seem possible. Growth that becomes untidy can be pruned to shape at any time, but is probably best done during the summer months when severed pieces can be cut up into sections and used for propagating new plants.

A peat and sand mix should be used for inserting cuttings in and a warm propagator will greatly improve chances of success.

BELOW:
Maranta leuconeura 'Kerchoveana' is a most striking plant, the leaves of which stand upright at nightfall. The pale grey-green leaves have distinctive dark blotches. It is a useful plant for placing as a foil at the base of large flowering plants.

Mimosa pudica**

Sensitive Plant 13°C (55°F). Brazil.
This pretty little plant is grown for its acutely sensitive ferny leaves and pink powder-puff blooms in July and August. When the compound leaves are touched during the day they react by drooping rapidly; the leaf stalks droop as well. They unfold their leaflets and resume their normal positions after a few minutes.

Set plants in a loam-based soil and support them with a short cane or two. Water freely during the growing season and feed weekly with liquid fertilizer. Grow in good light but shade from hot sunshine. Admit plenty of air if the tempetature rises above 18–20°C (64–70°F). Keep the air moist. Usually grown as an annual and discarded after flowering.

Raise new plants from seed in gentle heat in February or March.

Monstera*

Swiss Cheese Plant 10°C (50°F). Mexico.

Monstera deliciosa possesses all the qualities that are required of a good houseplant subject. Leaves are a rich green in colour and have a natural gloss to them which is heightened when plants are cleaned with a proprietary leaf cleaner. White oil used at a strength of approximately 15 ml (1 tbsp) to 3 litres (5 pints) of water will improve the look of most plants with glossy leaves, but soft new leaves should never be cleaned. It will also help to keep pests under control.

In ideal conditions the monstera will produce quite enormous leaves that, as well as being deeply serrated along their margins, will also become naturally perforated. Monstera plants will do better if the aerial roots that grow from the main stem can be directed into a container of water from which supplies will be drawn for the plant, thus reducing the need for too frequent watering of the mixture in the pot in which the roots of the plant are growing. The aerial roots can sometimes be directed into the soil, but if they present difficulties it would not be too harmful to a large plant for some aerial roots to be taken off with a sharp knife. For best results monsteras should enjoy conditions that are fairly moist, shaded from the sun and reasonably warm.

When potting plants on into larger pots, a mix comprised of equal parts loam-based mixture and sphagnum peat or clean leafmould should be used. Mature plants produce exquisite creamy-white inflorescences, the spathe part of which remains colourful for only a few days while the spadix in the centre develops into a rich-tasting fruit, which should be left until it is almost mushy ripe before it is eaten.

New plants are raised by removing the growing tips with one mature leaf and inserting them in a peaty mix.

Peperomia**

13°C (55°F). Tropical America.

The keen indoor plantsman may in time collect quite a number of peperomias, but not all of them are suitable as houseplants, or very attractive as potted plants for that matter. So a certain amount of selectivity is needed, and it will usually be found that those plants favoured by the commercial growers are, in fact, the better plants for room decoration. Possibly the most popular are varieties of *P. magnoliae-folia*, of compact habit and producing thick, fleshy leaves that are an attractive cream and green in colour in the variegated forms. Similar in colour is *P. glabella* 'Variegata' which has small light green and white leaves and is of trailing habit, so useful for many locations indoors where more erect plants would be out of place. These two will require a reasonably light position in the room and a watering programme that errs on the dry side. However, provide a humid atmosphere from April to September, syringing the leaves twice a day when hot.

RIGHT:
Monstera pertusa *is one of the largest foliage house-plants, and consequently very popular for offices and public buildings. Fortunately, when in a small container its growth can be reduced and controlled.*

BELOW:
Peperomia caperata *is one of the best known peperomias, with white spike-like flowers on red stems. However, peperomias are chiefly grown for their attractive leaves. This plant can be increased by stem-and-leaf cuttings.*

As peperomias go, a larger plant that may well suit the more selective purchaser is *P. obtusifolia*, of which there are a number of varieties. Leaves are a purplish green in colour and are about 10 cm (4 in) in length — mature plants attain a height of some 30 cm (1 ft).

All the peperomias do well in loamless or very peaty mixtures.

All the foregoing may be propagated between April and August, either from top cuttings with two or three leaves attached, or a single leaf with a piece of stem attached.

Peperomia caperata and *P. hederaefolia* are both propagated by using individual leaves with petiole attached and inserting far enough for the leaves to remain erect in a peat and sand mixture. The first mentioned has small dark green purple-tinted leaves that are crinkled and heart-shaped, while the latter has leaves of similar shape, a quilted texture and an overall metallic-grey colouring.

Philodendron*/**
15°C (60°F). Tropical America.

Many and fine species are in this genus, some quite majestic and much too large for the average living room, while others like the Sweetheart Plant, *P. scandens*, with small heart-shaped leaves and habit, are ideal for room decoration. *P. scandens* can be encouraged to trail or climb depending on requirements.

All philodendrons will appreciate the maximum amount of humidity that can be provided, and this will mean use of a larger container filled with peat for plunging plant pots, and regular spraying over of the foliage.

Philodendron hastatum has much larger green leaves that are arrow-shaped, and will develop into a plant of substantial size if a stout support can be provided. In fact, with all members of the aroid family it will considerably improve their performance if a thick layer of sphagnum moss can be wired to the supporting stake —

BELOW:
This Philodendron lacerum, *a distinctive member of the philodendron family, is supported by a sphagnum moss-covered stake, forming an attractive foil to the distinctively shaped leaves. Occasionally, the sphagnum-covered stake will need to be dampened, as otherwise the moss tends to flake off.*

this will encourage the aerial roots to work their way into the moss, so helping the plant to obtain additional moisture. The moss should be maintained in moist conditions by regular spraying, or by using a watering can to moisten the moss from the top of the support. When doing this, be careful not to get the soil in the pot too wet. Ideally you should endeavour to provide conditions that are warm, moist and shaded — in bright sunlight plants take on a very hard, less green appearance that is not so attractive.

Besides the upright growing types of philodendron there are numerous plants of much more squat habit that are more suitable for some locations. Many of the latter grow from short trunks that become most attractive as some of the lower leaves are naturally shed.

Architecturally speaking, one of the finest of the lower-growing philodendrons is *P. wendlandii*, which produces leaves that radiate away from the centre of the plant in the shape of a shuttlecock — alas it is ever in short supply as most of the larger types of philodendron forever seem to be.

Almost all the smaller-leaved plants may be propagated from individual leaves with a piece of stem attached, while the larger-leaved ones are raised from seed.

Pilea*/**
Aluminium Plant 10–13°C (50–55°F). Indo-China and Tropical America.
The most well known of the pileas is *Pilea cadierei*, the Aluminium Plant, whose leaves are splashed with shining white between the veins. It was discovered in the Vietnamese forests and introduced to France in 1938. All the plants that have been grown since have originated from a single plant.

Pilea muscosa is a rather bushy little plant growing to a height of 28 cm (11 in), that is not unlike a fern at first sight. It has small pale to mid-green leaves and inconspicuous tufts of yellow-green flowers. The common name of Artillery Plant results from the manner in which seed pods explode when ripe and scatter seed in all directions.

Pilea cadierei needs regular feeding to retain its attractive silver-grey colouring. Also regular pinching out of leading shoots is necessary in order to keep plants compact.

All pileas on sale commercially may be increased by means of cuttings with very little difficulty — quite a few will also seed themselves in every direction if, for example, they are growing on gravel on greenhouse staging. In fact, the ease of propagation should encourage you to adopt the practice of disposing of old and

38

overgrown plants and replacing them with freshly-rooted new ones periodically.

Rhoicissus rhomboidea*
Grape Ivy 10°C (50°F). South Africa.
A natural climbing plant growing to at least 1·2 m (4 ft) that will adapt to many different locations, but prefers reasonable warmth, light shade, moderate watering and regular feeding while in active growth. Stems are woody in older plants and leaves are tri-lobed and an attractive glossy green. Provide canes or a trellis for the tendrils to cling to.

Pot on annually in April until they are in 23 cm (9 in) pots.

Cuttings are prepared in April or May from pieces of stem with two leaves attached — several cuttings should be put in each small pot to provide plants of full appearance.

Sansevieria*
Mother-in-law's Tongue 10°C (50°F). West Africa.
The erect sword-like leaves, dark green with mottled grey transverse bands of S. trifasciata, grow to 30–45 cm (12–18 in) and make this species a popular feature of indoor plant gardens. The variety S. t. 'Laurentii', with creamy-yellow margins to the leaves, is the form usually seen.

A loam-based soil mix is suitable for this semi-succulent, and like other succulents it should be allowed to dry out completely between waterings. Keep dry during the winter. A sunny or lightly shaded position will suit it well as it is a tough plant which will thrive in almost any light conditions. Feed established plants every three or four months during the growing season.

Most varieties can be propagated by leaf cuttings, but in the case of S. t. 'Laurentii' this method is unsuccessful as the offspring will lack the characteristic yellow strips. The variety should therefore be increased by severing underground stolons from the parent plant when they have formed two or three leaves.

Saxifraga stolonifera* (syn. S. sarmentosa)
Mother of Thousands 10°C (50°F). China.
Ideal indoor hanging plants that are better in small pots with wire supports rather than in larger more conventional hanging baskets. Close inspection shows that the rounded leaves are multi-coloured, but the overall impression is a rather dull-grey colouring. Small starry flowers are produced in July and August.

New plants are propagated from the perfectly shaped young plantlets that are produced on slender red stems by the parent plant — hence the common name.

BELOW:
Saxifraga sarmentosa *is often known as* Saxifraga stolonifera. *It is easy to grow, preferring a light and cool room, but not direct sunshine. It thrives in small pots, but take care not to allow the soil to dry out.*

RIGHT:
Schefflera actinophylla is highly distinctive, with leaves originating from the same point on each leaf stem. It is a plant that needs reasonable warmth with light shade. Keep the plant moist, giving regular feeds with a liquid fertilizer.

BELOW:
Scindapsus aureus or Devil's Ivy has exceedingly handsome foliage but needs some form of support. It delights in warmth and plenty of humidity, and thrives when climbing up a damp sphagnum support. Nip out the tip of each leading shoot each winter to reduce its natural tendency to climb and ramble.

Schefflera actinophylla**

Umbrella Plant 10–13°C (50–55°F). Australia. Elegant plants with large palmate shiny green leaves that are seen to best effect when grown as individual specimens rather than in a group. Needs reasonable warmth, light shade in summer and moderate humidity, and must have a mixture with a loam base; keep the soil moist throughout the year. Give a dilute liquid feed once every month in summer.

May be propagated either from seed in February or from stem cuttings.

Scindapsus**

Devil's Ivy 10–13°C (50–55°F). South East Asia.

Natural climbers, these are akin to philodendrons but slightly more difficult. *S. aureus* has heart-shaped leaves that are attractively cream and green variegated. The variety 'Marble Queen' has almost entirely white leaves, and 'Golden Queen' is almost completely yellow. Warm, moist and shaded conditions are essential, although a well-lit spot is preferred in

winter. A very peaty compost is best.

New plants can be raised from individual leaves with a piece of stem attached.

Tolmiea menziesii*
Pick-a-back Plant. Hardy. North America.
A curiosity plant that produces perfectly-shaped young plants at the base of older parent leaves – young plants can be removed when large enough and propagated with little difficulty.

Plants form into compact mounds of hairy green foliage and grow to a height of 15 cm (6 in). Pot between September and March, repot annually in March or April, and water freely in the growing period. You can expect few problems of care and attention.

Tradescantia*
Wandering Jew 10°C (50°F). Tropical America.
The vast majority of the great many tradescantias that are available are easy to care for, easy to propagate from almost any piece of stem, and are seen at their best when several plants are put into a hanging basket and given light and airy conditions in which they can develop.

The ovate leaves, closely set on the trailing stems, are striped in various colours. Flowers are three-petalled and basically triangular in outline. Avoid blazing sun, but in good light plants will have much more pleasingly coloured variegation. After two or three growing seasons, plants should be disposed of and replaced with more vigorous young plants.

When propagating put several pieces in each small pot and remove the growing tips of young plants regularly to encourage bushiness.

Zebrina pendula
10°C (50°F). Mexico.
Closely related to the tradescantias, this is a very beautiful, easily grown plant, that can be used for much the same purposes. The upper surfaces of its leaves are silvery, edged green, with a purple centre stripe and bright purple on their undersides, which colours are appreciably enhanced if the plant is kept a little on the dry side. Z. purpusii has dark-mauve, rather large leaves.

ABOVE:
Trailing plants are very useful, especially as hanging plants in containers. The attractive array of plants seen here are (in the top position and moving clockwise): Tradescantia fluminensis 'Quicksilver', Zebrina pendula, Tradescantia fluminesis 'Aurea', Tradescantia fluminensis 'Variegata', *and* Zebrina purpusii.

41

Palms and ferns

Palms and ferns are two groups of plants that are often neglected by houseplant enthusiasts. There are plenty of varieties which are easy to grow, and they can bring an interesting variety of shape and form to any collection of houseplants. They will make an especially attractive focal point in a modern home, where a good specimen can form a majestic centrepiece.

Many gardeners are deterred from trying palms because of their association with tropicel climates. Also, they often take several years to reach their full beauty, and consequently tend to be expensive to buy. But no one should be deterred from growing these elegant plants, for just one fine specimen strategically placed in the home will add considerable interest and well repay its cost.

Provided a winter temperature of about 10°C (50°F) can be maintained, palms are not difficult to grow, and they can be surprisingly tough. Because they are slow growing, it will be many years before they outgrow their usefulness in the home – it will be a long time before most species reach 1·5–1·8 m (5–6 ft) in the restricted conditions of a pot. Ideally, they should be planted in special palm pots, which are deeper than normal plant pots.

Unlike ferns, most species appreciate good light, though some will grow well in light shade.

Two of the best palms to start with are *Chameadorea elegans* (sometimes sold as *Neanthe balla* and popularly known as the Parlour Palm), a small plant that will only reach about 120 cm (4 ft) after many years, and *Howea forsteriana*, the Kentia Palm. Both should be positioned out of direct sunlight, with frequent watering during the summer. Palms will benefit from their leaves being sponged or sprayed occasionally, as a dry atmosphere tends to cause browning of the leaf tips.

Ferns are much more plentiful and less costly to buy than palms, and they should find a place in every home. Indeed, ferns are good plants to collect, for they are long-lived and will thrive in positions other plants would not.

One of the most popular and widely available species is the Maidenhead Fern (*Adiantum capillus-veneris*), which is a favourite with florists. In fact, most ferns have finely divided leaves, but there are also broad-leaved types such as the Bird's Nest Fern (*Asplenium nidus*), which forms a rosette of broad, glossy light green fronds, and the interesting Stag Horn Fern (*Platycerium bifurcatum*) with its antler-like blades. There are even variegated ferns, such as the very attractive *Pteris ensiformis* 'Victoriae', which has white veins and dark green serrated margins.

Ferns will thrive in shady place positions, though some of the tropical species will tolerate light, provided they are not in direct sunshine. The most important need is for a moist atmosphere and soil that is always damp but not waterlogged. Because of the humidity, ferns are a good choice for bathrooms.

An acid compost containing plenty of peat is necessary, and whenever possible soft water should be used for watering.

Most ferns are fairly hardy, and the tropical types can be grown quite satisfactorily in a centrally-heated home, provided humidifiers are used to keep the air moist. All ferns appreciate an overhead spray once or twice a week.

Ferns are ideal candidates for Wardian cases. These are glass containers, usually rectangular in shape and with an ornamental lid, that were originated in 1892 by the London physician Nathanial Ward. Plants in these containers transpired water vapour from their leaves, which condensed on the glass and returned to the soil to moisten it and water the roots of the plants.

Adiantum*

Maidenhair Fern 7°C (45°F). Sub-tropical and temperate zones.

Ferns are nothing if not varied in leaf form, and you can be forgiven for not realizing that the Maidenhair is a fern. The rounded leaflets (pinnae) and thin wiry stems are quite untypical of ferns, but the clue is in the clusters of raised brown spots on the underside of the leaves of adult plants — these contain the fern spores. They are *not* a sign of disease or a form of scale insect!

Many species of Maidenhair ferns are similar in appearance, having wiry black leaf stalks growing out of a quickly spreading horizontal rhizome. *A. capillus-veneris* (Venus'-hair or Maidenhair Fern) grows to a height of 20–30 cm (8–12 in) and the leaf stalks carry many branched fronds of delicate fan-shaped pinnae which are pale green in colour. In mature plants, the undersides of the pinnae are edged with brown sori (clusters of sporangia), giving extra colour to the fern.

A. cuneatum (syn. *A. raddianum*) is a Brazilian species very similar in appearance to *A. capillus-veneris* although a little larger, growing to 50 cm (1⅔ ft) in height. The pinnae are also coarser. However, it is not always easy to distinguish between the two as there are several cultivars of *A. cuneatum* which vary in size and also in colour from yellow-green to dark green.

The Rosy Maidenhair, *A. hispidulum,* is a species different in appearance, the young foliage being reddish-brown in colour changing to medium green with age. The petioles are covered with dark brown scales and the plant grows to about 30 cm (1 ft) in height. The frond blade looks more like the spread fingers of a hand, not branched nearly as much as in the other Maidenhair species, and pinnae are longer.

All the maidenhairs require plenty of humidity; this is absolutely essential for their fine, delicate fronds, otherwise they turn brown at the edges and wither up completely in a day or two. Misting them every day, and providing humidity from containers or humidifiers is vital.

Direct sunlight should be avoided; however, the plant should not be placed in a dark corner. A north or east-facing windowsill is ideal.

Maidenhair ferns are easily increased by cutting the rhizome into pieces, each with a few fronds and roots. Pot these into a peaty compost in a smaller pot.

Asparagus fern*

This 'fern' with feathery leaves, so often used in corsages and wedding bouquets, is not in fact a true fern, but a flowering plant related to the vegetable. The popular asparagus 'ferns' have been known for years as *A. plumosus* (the feathery upright kind) and *A. sprengeri* (often grown as a trailer), but these have now been renamed by botanists as *A. setaceus* and *A. densiflorus* respectively. Cultural hints are given in the chapter on foliage houseplants.

Asplenium**

Spleenwort 13°C (55°F) min. Australia/New Zealand/Far East.

Two main species are grown, perhaps the most popular being *Asplenium nidus*, the Bird's Nest Fern. As with many bromeliads, this tropical fern is an epiphyte, living on the trees of the rain forests of Africa and Asia, and also in Australia.

Its fronds are totally unlike the conventional fern, as they consist of a single segment forming a leaf blade like that of an ordinary flowering plant, glossy and light green in colour. They form a kind of funnel-shaped rosette, for the same reason that the bromeliads do, and can

become enormous — up to 20 cm (8 in) wide and 90 cm (3 ft) long, in the right conditions of warmth and moisture.

Warmer and more humid conditions give the larger plant. Sori forming a fishbone-like pattern on undersides of mature blades shower a mass of light brown spores on to lower fronds.

Give it a peaty compost and the occasional spray so that water runs down the leaves into the centre. Use a nitrogenous fertilizer while growing. It is an epiphyte and so will grow in peaty compost bound on to bark, hung from a support.

The other species, *A. bulbiferum*, has deeply serrated pinnae spread out in a triangular shape from a black petiole and rachis to make a frond which can be up to 60 cm (2 ft) in length and 23 cm (9 in) wide. Fertile pinnae produce sporangia on narrow segments of the serrations while sterile pinnae have broader segments. Inter-mixing of fertile and sterile pinnae on the same frond gives added interest to the shape.

The appearance of this fern can be rather bizarre for plantlets that are miniature editions of the parent plant grow from bulbils produced on the upper surface of the pinnae. Thus new plants are easily propagated by placing a pinna with bulbils on to a moist peaty potting mix. Roots are quickly formed and the plantlets soon grow independently.

ABOVE:
The Bird's Nest Fern, Asplenium nidus, has attractive glossy light-green fronds which unfurl from the centre of the rosette. Superb specimens of this plant grow up to 1 m (1 yd), across in warm and humid conditions.

45

Chamaedorea elegans* (syn. *Neanthe bella*)
Parlour Palm 13°C (55°F). Mexico.
If you want a tall, graceful plant for your living-room, then a palm is usually a good choice. Their arching stems and fronds are elegant and airy, and chamaedorea is one of the smaller palms with these qualities. Each leaf blade is wider and shorter than those of many palms, giving it a more obviously pinnate look, and it does not very often grow much taller than about 60 cm (2 ft). It is, in fact, a natural miniature palm that is ideal for smaller rooms, for bottle gardens, and dish gardens.

It is the only one likely to produce flowers — small yellow blobs dotted along the flower stem in a kind of plume which, if they set, are followed by pea-like, shiny fruits. The hotter and sunnier the weather is during summer, the more likely is chamaedorea to produce these flowers, usually when three or more years old.

In common with all the palms, the best method of propagation is by means of seed. Seed is sown in shallow peat beds that are maintained at a temperature of not less than 20°C (70°F), and allowed to grow on in the bed until plants are several cm tall before potting them individually in small pots of open mixture.

Chrysalidocarpus lutescens* (syn. *Areca lutescens*)
Butterfly Palm 15°C (60°F). India.
Lutescens means yellow, which refers to the yellow stems and leaves which results in a most attractive and desirable plant. At first sight these plants have the appearance of palms that are suffering as a result of some iron deficiency. However, the Butterfly Palm has much finer foliage and is altogether more delicate in appearance than *Howea forsteriana*. An attractive feature of this plant is to witness the slow process of new leaves opening – leaves are delicate-ly joined at their tips giving the leaf a skeletonized appearance prior to fully expanding.

This highly attractive plant has an almost aristocratic appearance and can easily dominate an unwanted area of a room, or conversely, it can be positioned to compliment a room's decor.

Cocos (Syagrus) weddeliana*
15°C (60°F). Cocos Islands.
One of the most delicate and compact of all the palms, the cocos has slender fronds that are dark green above, glaucous on the undersides. It retains a dwarf stature of about 30 cm (1 ft) for several years and when established will go on for at least two years in the same pot. Some care is needed, such as a humid atmosphere, freely circulating air and good light out of direct sun. A loam-based compost is preferable, kept moist in summer.

Cycas revoluta
Sago Palm 15°C (60°F). China.
One of the oldest and, surely, one of the most majestic plants in cultivation. In time the plant develops a substantial trunk, which adds considerably to the general appearance, to a height of at least 1·8 m (6 ft). Leaves are dark green and stiff and individual segments are narrow, bending slightly at their tips. Not a plant for the impatient gardener, as only a very few leaves are produced annually and growth rate is painfully slow. It needs plenty of moisture and water and you should use a loam-based mixture.

Cyrtomium falcatum* (syn. *Polystichum falcatum*)
Fish-tail Fern 7°C (45°F) min. South East Asia.
The upright fronds can grow to 60 cm (2 ft) long and they have silver furry scale covering their petioles. About 12 pairs of dark green glossy leathery pinnae form the blade, each pinna being similar in shape to a holly leaf. Sporangia are scattered irregularly over the underside of the pinnae and first appear as very small green spots changing to light brown with maturity.

These ferns are said to be indestructible, but perhaps a better description would be that they are more tolerant than most to lower temperatures and humidity. They also tolerate draughts and smoke quite well.

Because these ferns grow satisfactorily with a degree of neglect, that does not mean they will not benefit from proper care and attention. Warmth, shade and humidity suit them best, and a weak liquid feed occasionally during the summer will keep them growing strongly.

Leaves will die naturally at intervals, and these should simply be removed. Water plentifully during the summer months, ideally with soft water, but only sparingly in winter.

Propagate by dividing an old plant in the spring, and potting the pieces in a fibrous, acid compost. Do not pot too firmly. Plants can also be raised from spores, and these sometimes fall and germinate spontaneously.

RIGHT:
The Butterfly Palm (Chrysalidocarpus) *has highly attractive foliage. It is a palm with a more delicate appearance than* Howea forsteriana, *and will bring a stateliness to any home.*

Davallia**

Squirrel's Foot Fern 5°C (41°F) min. Far East.
It is the furry rhizomes of *D. bullata* which give
this fern its common name. They spread quickly
and a mass of dwarf fronds shoots up from
them. The blade is triangular in outline, dark
green and the pinnae are deeply cut. A rhizome
tip when laid on moist potting mix will root
quickly and then rapidly divide to cover a small
hanging basket. It is a very tolerant plant, not
objecting to the dryer atmosphere of a modern
home and even liking a little sunlight.

The Hare's Foot Fern, *D. canariensis* is a small
popular species with thick rhizomes that are pale
brown in colour. The leathery fronds are mid-
green and finely cut.

D. fijiensis has a much freer habit of growth.
The fronds are larger, lighter in colour and
appear more delicate and finely cut.

Howea** (syn. *Kentia*)

Kentia Palm 10–13°C (50–55°F). Lord Howe
Islands.
Howeas are palms from Lord Howe Island in
the Pacific. Kentia is the name of the capital,
and the plants have until recently had *Kentia*
as botanic name. One species is still called the
Kentia Palm as a common name.

A howea is one of the palms with feathery
leaves, very graceful and eventually growing
into a large, imposing plant several metres tall.
In natural conditions, when young, the plants
grow in considerable shade, so do not worry
too much about light. Even when more mature
they will be happy in some shade.

Howea forsteriana has a more erect habit of
growth than *H. belmoreana*, and for that reason
is better suited to most indoor locations. Leaves
are a rich, dark green in colour, but are surprisingly susceptible to damage if cleaned with
chemical concoctions that appear to cause little
or no harm to plants that would seem much
more vulnerable.

When potting howeas on from one pot to
another larger one it is very important that a
good layer of crocks should be placed in the
bottom of the new pot before introducing
mixture, as this will ensure that drainage is
sharp and that the mixture does not become
waterlogged. The addition of coarse leafmould
to a standard potting mixture will be of considerable benefit in assisting plants to grow
more freely indoors. When potting, the mixture
should be made fairly firm. In a medium that is
badly aerated there will be a tendency for the
mixture to turn sour with the result that plants
take on a generally hard, less green appearance,
and in time will result in browning of tips of
leaves and eventual loss of leaves.

Except for the fact that leaves are narrower
it is difficult to detect the difference between
H. belmoreana and *H. forsteriana* in the early
stages of growth. However, as *belmoreana* ages,
the midrib of the leaf arches and the plant
adopts a more drooping appearance which is
not unattractive in larger plants.

LEFT:
*The Squirrel's Foot Fern,
Davallia bullata, is shown to
perfection in this illustration.
It is a very tolerant fern, not
objecting to the dryer
atmosphere of many modern
homes. It will even tolerate a
little sunshine.*

BELOW:
*Many palms are exceedingly
stately and add greatly to a
room setting. Here, Howea
belmoreana (on the right)
and Chamaedorea elegans
(on the table) create a cool
and sedate environment.
Occasionally it will be
necessary to wipe the leaves
with a damp cloth.*

Humata tyermannii**

Bear's-Foot Fern 7°C (45°F) min. West Africa. Small rhizomes covered with white furry scales divide frequently and a frond is sent up every 5–8 cm (2–3 in). When young the frond is rosy-green turning to very dark green with age. The blade shape is like a long pointed triangle 15–23 cm/6–9 in high and up to 13 cm/5 in wide at the base. The pinnae are finely cut. It is best to provide a fairly large potting mix surface for this fern as it is a quick grower under good conditions.

Lygodium japonicum**

Climbing Fern 7°C (45°F) min. Japan.
The petiole and rachis are very long and wiry, climbing by twining round a trellis or pillar. Oppositely paired pinnae grow out from the rachis and are yellow-green to medium green in colour. Fertile pinnae are long and tapering with serrated edges, the lobes of which carry the sori; sterile pinnae are similar in form but with more and deeper serrations. The plants can be divided in March or April.

When grown on a windowsill, a climbing fern is liable to twine through light curtains or venetian blinds unless precautions are taken.

Nephrolepis*

Ladder Fern 10°C (50°F) min. Tropics and subtropics.
The graceful Ladder Fern, *N. exaltata*, is deservedly popular; it is easily grown, elegant and feathery, available in all sorts of decorative forms, and especially pretty in a hanging basket. It is very similar to *N. cordifolia* but much larger and coarser, with pale green fronds growing up to 2 m (6½ ft) long. The blade tapers at base and tip and looks somewhat like a ladder in silhouette.

Many cultivars of *N. exaltata* have been produced by cross-breeding; most are of interest to indoor growers, the greatly divided blades giving cristate forms. *N. exaltata* 'Bostoniensis' (Boston Fern), with broad fronds and fast-growing, was a very early mutant and the many later mutations have provided us with modern cultivars that are easier to grow in present-day living rooms. 'Rooseveltii Plumosa' has very wavy segments; 'Whitmanii' is commonly called

BELOW:
This Lygodium japonicum *thrives when grown in enclosed, spacious surroundings.*

48

the Lace Fern, a description in itself; 'Elegantissima' is similar to 'Whitmanii' but more upright. Occasionally a frond will revert to the original single segment form and it should be removed immediately. Often spores from these cultivars are infertile and then the form can only be propagated by runners.

The Sword Fern, *N. cordifolia*, has very short petioles which carry narrow blades cut to the rachis, forming segments, the whole frond growing to a length of 60 cm (2 ft). The colour is light green. Large plants are best grown in hanging baskets or on pedestals, for the mixed upright and pendulous fronds show to advantage from a low angle. In the cultivar 'Plumosa' all the segment tips are fringed.

Nephrolepis are propagated by runners growing from the top of a rhizome; the runners root quickly when in contact with a moist potting mix.

RIGHT:
The Stag Horn Fern,
Platycerium bifurcatum, *is
totally unlike most people's
idea of a fern. Mature plants
are often up to 1·83 m (6 ft)
across and usually suspended
from the roof. When small,
however, single plants can be
grown in a pot or attached to
a piece of bark padded with
sphagnum moss.*

BELOW:
The Button Fern, Pellaea
rotundifolia, *is an
interesting fern to grow
as it forms a low spreading
mat. It is also a fairly
tolerant plant and is not
difficult to grow.*

Pellaea**

Button Fern 7°C (45°F) min. New Zealand.
Pellaea rotundifolia the Cliff-Brake or Button
Fern has brown hairy scales covering a wiry
petiole and rachis which has about 20 pairs of
alternately placed pinnae. The small roundish
pinnae are dark green above, light green below
and a little leathery. Fronds up to 50 cm (20 in)
long form a low spreading mat so that this fern

is useful in temporary plant arrangements as
ground cover for it is fairly tolerant as to conditions and able to utilize any humidity from the
surrounding potting mix. Sori form on the
underside margins of a pinna but do not meet
at the apex and are light brown in colour.

Unlike the previous fern, *P. viridis* is an African species of upright and bushy habit. Fronds
grow up to 75 cm (2½ ft) long; rachides are
green when young turning shining black with
age and blades of bright green spear-shaped
pinnae. It is unusual for a fern to grow well in
very bright light, but this species does well
under the lower intensity of fluorescent lighting.
It needs a winter temperature of 10°C (50°F).

Phoenix**

Date Palm 10–13°C (50–55°F). South East
Asia/Canary Islands.
Phoenix dactylifera is the commercial date palm
of North Africa, but is seldom offered as a potted
plant. Although in short supply, the two varieties that you are likely to come across as potted
plants are *P. canariensis* and *P. roebelenii*, the
latter from South East Asia. Should there be a
choice, the latter is much more graceful and is,
therefore, a much more desirable plant for room

decoration. Both are planted throughout the tropics as decorative trees, but they take many, many years to reach maturity when their roots are confined to plant pots. In many locations the slow growing plant of architectural merit, as these two are, is much more rewarding than plants that are forever in need of replacement. Both plants have stiff leaves and robust appearance, and are not difficult to care for in reasonable conditions – but avoid having the soil saturated for long periods.

Platycerium bifurcatum** (syn. *P. alcicorne*)
Stag Horn Fern 10°C (50°F) min. Australia.
There are many platycerium species, and all grow as true epiphytes on the branches and in the forks of trees.

The Stag Horn Fern is totally unlike one's idea of a normal fern. The frond consists of an entire, rather thick, leaf-like structure, which divides towards the end into a fork-like arrangement that gives it its common name. The fronds are light green, but covered with a grey bloom when young, which gradually disappears as they age.

These showy fronds are the fertile ones. The sterile fronds are the sheath-like ones which form the base of the plant, and which gradually become brown and papery with age, overlapping the edges of the container. The fertile fronds grow from the centre of this mass of folded, fan-like sheaths.

In the home a Stag Horn may be grown in a pot or attached to bark padded with sphagnum moss; either way, in time sterile fronds will cover the holder. It should be watered by immersing pot or bark periodically, preferably in rainwater.

To keep its beautiful velvety appearance, inquisitive fingers should not be allowed to touch the fronds as once removed the 'velvet' will never return.

Polypodium aureum (syn. *Phlebodium aureum*)
Hare's- or Rabbit's-foot Fern 7°C (45°F) min. West Indies.
Good specimens will grow fronds 1 m (3¼ ft) tall, although young plants of 40 cm (16 in) are very decorative. The frond has a light green petiole turning brown with age, a blue- to yellow-green blade made of single and opposite pinnae each up to 13 cm (5 in) long. In some cultivars the pinnae have wavy edges. Each frond arises from a thick silver to brown furry rhizome that gives this fern its common name. The rhizome is surface-creeping and will follow the contour of a container. Dead fronds drop away leaving a scar on the rhizome rather like a small footprint.

Pteris*
Ribbon Fern 10–13°C (50–55°F) min. Mediterranean/Tropical Asia.
The pteris group of plants are ferns needing warmth or tropical conditions; none of them is hardy but *Pteris cretica* (the Ribbon Fern) and *P. ensiformis* are the least tender and easiest to grow. *Pteris* was the word used by the Greek physician Dioscorides for a fern, and comes from the Greek *pteron*, a wing, referring to the frond shape.

The Ribbon Fern, *P. cretica*, has a very short rhizome common to all pteris so that growth is in clumps with very many fronds arising from a crown. *P. cretica*, about 50 cm (1⅔ ft) tall, has longish pointed pinnae with serrated edges that only show on the sterile pinnae because the sori are protected by the pinna edge curling back. It is medium green in colour and quite tough.

There are many cultivars, all more interesting in shape or colour. *P. c.* 'Albolineata', as the name implies, has a white central line running the length of each pinna; 'Rivertoniana' has pinnae with elongated segments growing irregularly from the margins; 'Wilsonii' and 'Wimsettii' both have heavily crested tips to their pinnae.

Pteris ensiformis 'Victoriae' is grown much more often than the type. It is a most attractive plant with short bushy sterile fronds having pinnae with white central veins banded by dark green serrated margins. Fertile fronds are taller, up to 50 cm (1⅔ ft), with very slender long pinnae on which the serrations only show at the tips where the margins stop curling back over the sori.

Shade is necessary for the variegated forms, as they lose their white markings in a light place, but the others can be grown in a moderately well-lit place.

The Trembling Fern, *P. tremula*, is a quickly-growing fern that can reach over 1 m (3 ft) if given the opportunity. However, young plants of 30–40 cm (12–16 in) are useful for grouping with other pteris species, the yellow-green foliage making a perfect foil for the darker greens. The feathery blade is triangular when seen in silhouette, and the pinnae have very deeply cut serrations.

LEFT:
Pteris ensiformis 'Victoriae' is a much grown fern, with very attractive short and bushy sterile fronds having pinnae with white central veins banded by dark green serrated margins. It is a fern especially suited to an attractive plant holder that blends with the foliage.

Flowering plants

No matter how many interesting foliage plants there are in a home, it is still enhanced by a few spectacular flowering species. A well-shaped azalea or a cyclamen covered in bloom will seldom fail to attract attention, while popular plants like saintpaulias (African Violets) and impatiens (Busy Lizzies) have a following all of their own.

The most readily available flowering houseplants have gained wide recognition because experience has shown they are good indoors, but it is well worth searching out some of the less widely grown plants as many of them are equally good, and the less common kinds do add interest to the home.

It is well worth raising some of your own plants from seed. It's always satisfying, and many kinds can be grown quite easily – especially if you have a greenhouse in which to start them. Many primulas, impatiens, calceolarias, cinerarias, the attractive climbing or trailing *Thunbergia alata* (Black-eyed Susan) and the gay and slightly fragrant *Exacum affine*, are just some that can be grown from seed.

Included in the following list of flowering plants are those grown primarily for their fruit or berries, such as the Calamodin Orange (*Citrus mitis*) and the Winter Cherry (*Solanum capsicastrum*), both of which can be grown from seed.

If time and space are limited, it is probably best to concentrate on growing winter-flowering houseplants, as indoor flowers are always most appreciated when the garden's bare.

Plants need not be tender or uncommon to qualify as flowering houseplants – the common Pot Marigold (*Calendula officinalis*) and clarkia both provide indoor colour in the spring from an autumn sowing. And of course the hardy hydrangea makes a wonderfully impressive plant indoors.

Flowering houseplants are not as easy to grow as most foliage plants, as light is usually much more critical. Most need good light (preferably direct sunlight) to induce flowers, so keep them as close to the window as possible, though some light shading may be necessary on the hottest days. If there's no room on the windowsill, try to position them on a table or plant stand as near as possible to the light. If you have a greenhouse where flowering plants can spend a few days from time to time they will be all the better for it.

The amount of light received each day affects the flowering period of some plants – common examples being chrysanthemums and poinsettias. The time of flowering can be brought forward or delayed by the amount of light received, and this should be borne in mind if artificial light cabinets are used to display plants.

If buds start to fall without opening, the cause is probably draughts or lack of humidity. A moist atmosphere is important for all plants, and it is particularly crucial as buds are forming. At this stage an overhead spray will help, though once the flowers open it is best to create a moist atmosphere around the plant by standing the pot in another container holding moist pebbles or peat.

Be sure to remove dead flower heads regularly, complete with stem, it keeps the plant looking tidy and it helps to prevent diseases encouraged by decaying flowers. If the flowerless stems are left on the plant they will develop a form of rot called botrytis.

Staking large flowerheads will also be necessary, especially for such plants as hydrangeas. With these, it is best to put a small split-bamboo stake in the centre of the pot, and with raffia or a thin and light-coloured string tie each separate bloom to the stake – looping it around a leaf-joint just below each flowerhead.

Achimenes**

Hot Water Plant 13°C (55°F). Mexico.

The cultivated species and varieties of achimenes are pretty, upright or trailing flowering plants, which can be grown in pots, troughs or hanging baskets. You can expect them to flower from mid summer to early autumn. The main colours are shades of purple, blue, violet, and rose-pink, but there are also red, yellow and white varieties, whose flowers are generally smaller, and rather shy to appear.

Achimenes have been grown on cottage windowsills for at least 100 years – most were introduced in the early 1800s from Central and South America. For a long time it was thought that they had to be watered with hot water, hence the common name, but water at room temperature is quite warm enough.

When the plants have finished flowering in September, dry off the tubers and store in a frost-free place until they start to develop new growth.

New plants can be raised in a number of different ways: from seed sown early in the year, from cuttings or by splitting up the scaly rhizomes from which growth develops. Immersing the pot, in which the rhizome is contained, in warm water when starting dormant plant into growth in February will encourage plants to develop new growth more rapidly.

BELOW:
Achimenes, the Hot Water Plant, originated from Mexico. It produces masses of tubular or trumpet-shaped flowers in a succession throughout the summer months. It requires a light and airy position, and its roots need to be kept moist but not saturated.

Anthurium scherzerianum***

Flamingo Flower 13°C (55°F). Tropical South America.

The anthuriums are beautiful and unusual flowering plants, belonging to the same family as the Wild Cuckoo Pint, or Lords and Ladies, which grows in hedgerows. The flower consists of a brilliantly red or pink, sometimes white, spathe (like a single large petal) and a coiled or straight spadix, on a stem 30–60 cm (1–2 ft) above the shiny green, spear-shaped or heart-shaped leaves.

Although this plant may be brought into flower at almost any time of the year, it is at its best during the spring months. In common with all aroids it will do much better if the general conditions are moist and humid, with reasonable warmth. Conditions that are very hot with little moisture are almost as bad as those that are cold.

The growing medium should contain a high proportion of peat, and the plant pot should be plunged in a larger container that is filled with peat or moss and kept moist. Large lanceolate leaves are dark green in colour and not unattractive, but the principal feature of this plant is the brilliant scarlet flower with a curled spadix.

Although smaller flowers on short stalks will be adequately supported, if larger flowers need some form of support, a cane that is tied in position just under the flower will be ideal.

Older plants may be split up to produce new plants, but this is not very easy. Raise new plants in peat in warm conditions.

Aphelandra**

Zebra Plant 10°C (50°F). Tropical South America.

Not many of our flowering houseplants have the added advantage of possessing decorative foliage as well as spectacular blooms, but in the two most popular varieties of aphelandra we have just such plants. Both have green leaves with prominent white stripes; A. squarrosa 'Louisae' is free flowering and may attain a height of some 60 cm (2 ft), while A. dania is smaller and more compact with more silvery foliage, but is less free with the colourful yellow flower spikes that are the crowning feature of these two fine pot plants.

It is easy to forget that the plants we grow with such care in pots in the home may be large and vigorous in their natural terrain. The Zebra Plant, for instance, is a bushy evergreen shrub in Brazil, where it grows 1–2 m (3–6 ft) tall.

Aphelandras are usually seen for sale in early winter; buy one whose bracts have only just started to separate, so that it lasts in flower as long as possible. When you get it home, water it every day; the leaves will quickly wilt if the roots are short of water. Then they fall, and very shortly you are left with a bare stem and a tuft of leaves and flower at the top.

It likes humidity, too; spray it every two or three days. It is one of the plants which does very well in a group of plants, all giving off moisture and making their own local micro-climate.

A lot of the difficulty comes because aphe-

RIGHT:
*The Flamingo Flower
(Anthurium scherzerianum)
comes from tropical South
America, and may be
brought into flower at
almost any time of the year.
However, it is at its best in
spring. It delights in a
compost with plenty of
moisture-retentive peat.*

54

landras are introduced to the home in early winter, when the atmosphere is dry, and plants tend to become forgotten anyway. Zebra Plants are especially sensitive, so it really pays to keep an eye on them.

With both plants it is essential that the soil is kept permanently moist and that plants are regularly fed with a balanced liquid fertilizer — the amount recommended by the manufacturer can be slightly increased and no harm will be done. Aphelandra plants make a mass of roots, hence the need for extra feeding — it is also the reason for using a soil that is loam-based when potting plants into larger containers, annually in spring.

In summer, provide some shade from strong sunlight, but keep the plants away from draughts or they will lose their lower leaves. When the plants have finished flowering it is best to remove the dead flowers and to cut the main stem at the top of the plant back to the first pair of sound leaves, from the axils of which new growth will develop. When these new shoots have developed two pairs of leaves they can be removed and put individually in small pots filled with a peat and sand mix — in a heated propagating case they will root in six weeks.

Azalea indicum**
Indian Azaleas 10–15°C (50–60°F). China.
These tender azaleas, correctly known as *Rhododendron simsii* (Indian Azaleas), are grown out of doors during the summer months and under glass from autumn until flowering in December. They are often thought of as the aristocrats of the winter-flowering range of pot plants, laden with red, pink or white blooms.

When purchasing a plant it is important to look for one with an abundance of buds, as plants that are too backward may not flower satisfactorily indoors, while those that are too advanced in flower will give pleasure for a shorter length of time.

The most important requirements in order to succeed with azaleas indoors is to ensure that the mixture is kept permanently wet, not moist, as any drying out will result in foliage shrivelling and flowers wilting. The best way of watering is to plunge the plant pot in a bucket of rainwater. This is treatment that larger plants may also require two or three times each week. Indoors, good light and cool growing conditions are essential, as plants seldom do well in very hot, airless situations.

After flowering, plants may be put out in the garden for the summer months where they should be kept moist and sprayed over periodically. When potting use a mixture composed almost entirely of leafmould and peat or a proprietary lime-free peat mix. Propagate from cuttings taken with a piece of old wood (a heel) and about 8 cm (3 in) in length during the summer. Insert cuttings in equal parts sharp sand and peat and maintain a temperature in the region of 15°C (60°F) until the new plants are established.

Begonia**
10–15°C (50–60°F). South America.
The begonia family takes well to container cultivation in the home, and includes a very varied and attractive range of plants. Many begonias grow from tubers, some of which are completely dormant in winter, others are fibrous-rooted and can have shoots and stems all year, though growth is slower in winter. Some have extremely colourful leaves, particularly the *Begonia rex* hybrids. Some have massive, brilliantly coloured double, sometimes fimbriated flowers, others have small flowers, but in great quantities for many months, sometimes flowering continuously through the year. It is possible to have a beautiful display of pot plants all year round by just growing different species and hybrids of begonias.

The double-flowered begonias grown from tubers need plenty of water while growing, a good light but not sun, a humid atmosphere and feeding from early summer until autumn. In late autumn they will die down of their own accord and watering should be gradually decreased. The withered stems are completely removed and the tubers left dry but frost-free until late winter, then put into moist peat with the top just above the surface, in a temperature of about 15°C (60°F).

New shoots will appear from the top of the tuber, and when these are about 5 cm (2 in) tall, the tuber can be potted into fresh standard potting compost and a 13–15 cm (5–6 in) pot.

Begonias are often seen out of doors in summer as bedding plants, with a mass of small flowers, pink, red or white, with light-green or wine-red leaves. These are easily grown in pots, to flower from late spring until mid autumn, or through the winter — the 'Lorraine' begonias. A good light, but no or little direct sun, water most days, and feeding, will keep them flowering until dried off and rested.

Another small-flowered begonia, of quite a different type, with a tuber, is *B. sutherlandii*. This has masses of small orange flowers in a kind of Victorian fringe dangling down round the outside.

There is now a modern strain of flowering begonias, whose flower size is between the large hybrids and those just described. These are the German Rieger begonias, which are excellent indoor plants, flowering continuously from spring until well into winter. Red, orange and salmon are the colours, and 'Fireglow' is one of the best.

Mildew can be a trouble with begonias, in stuffy conditions, when plants are short of water at the roots.

Begonia glaucophylla is one of the many fibrous-rooted begonias that are excellent value both in respect of attractive foliage and colourful flowers. These are particularly suitable for hanging pots and baskets, as the thin, long stems droop naturally. Leaves are pale green and glossy with waved margins and darken as they mature. Clustered brick-red flowers are a

welcome sight during the month of February. Being a natural trailing plant it is seen at its best when several plants are put in a hanging basket during the summer to flower the following year. Use a peaty mixture when planting them and set in good light and keep evenly moist, especially while flowering. Increase plants by inserting pieces of stem with one or two leaves attached in a peat and sand mixture — a heated propagator will speed the rooting time.

Beloperone guttata*
Shrimp Plant 7°C (45°F). Mexico.
This is a gem of a plant that is forever in keen demand. Soft green leaves are produced on stiff, wiry stems that need no support until plants reach a height of some 45 cm (18 in). The flowering bracts are a rich shade of brown overlapping white and resemble shrimps — hence the common name. They appear almost continually throughout the year. However, it is better to force the plant to rest for a few weeks, in winter, otherwise it becomes weak and does not live long.

Plants can be pruned to shape after flowering in early spring, and throughout the growing season they will require regular feeding. Potting into a loam-based mixture with a little extra peat should not be neglected if larger plants are required.

To produce larger plants it will also help if the bracts on young plants are removed for the first few months; the plant will then put all its energy into producing more lush foliage.

Propagate from cuttings inserted in fresh peat in a propagator, and pot into gradually larger pots as plants fill their existing containers with roots.

Calendula officinalis*
Pot Marigold. Hardy. Southern Europe.
Pot marigolds in their many fine colours are excellent value as potted plants and are comparatively inexpensive to purchase. Indeed they are easily raised at home from seed sown in late summer or autumn. They require a cool, light place indoors, and the soil must at all times be kept moist.

Having finished flowering they should be disposed of, because they are annuals; however, if it is not too late in the year they can be planted out in the garden after careful deadheading and may then produce a second show of flowers.

LEFT:
Beloperone guttata, the Shrimp Plant, certainly lives up to its common name — the flowers closely resemble small shrimps. It is a plant that needs plenty of sunshine, regular watering, and feeding during the spring and summer. Prune straggly shoots in the spring to keep the plant in shape.

FAR LEFT:
Begonia 'Sugar Candy' is one of the tuberous begonias. Most tuberous begonias are summer- and autumn-flowering, with single or double flowers — some with frilled edges. They can range in colour from yellow, orange and red and pink to white.

Calceolaria

Slipper Flower 10–15°C (50–60°F). South America.

In common with the majority of flowering pot plants, the calceolaria abhors very hot conditions, and much prefers the cool room that is light and well-ventilated. It is important to keep plants moist at all times and to feed them well.

Small plants when first purchased will benefit if potted immediately into a loam-based mixture – this will reduce the need for feeding and encourage plants to retain their rich green colouring. Keep a watchful eye for greenfly and treat immediately.

Discard plants when they have finished flowering. Most calceolarias are of hybrid origin and have soft, slightly hairy leaves. The pouch-shaped flowers, borne in large clusters on top of the plants, are usually in shades of red, orange or yellow, and marked with contrasting colours.

ABOVE:
Calceolarias, the Slipper Flower, bear very distinctive pouch-like flowers in colours such as yellow and red. It is essential to feed the plants and to keep them well watered. Place them in a cool and well-ventilated room, free from draughts.

Campanula isophylla*

Bellflower 7°C (45°F). Italy.

The Italian bellflower is easy to grow, and is very satisfactory in hanging baskets.

There are two varieties that one may occasionally see offered for sale: *C. isophylla* 'Alba', and *C. isophylla* 'Mayi'. As the name suggests, the first mentioned has white flowers and is reasonably easy to care for, while the latter has pale blue flowers and variegated, heart-shaped leaves; it is a trifle more difficult to manage. Both may be increased by means of cuttings

inserted in a peat and sand mixture in spring.

The white form is a particularly fine plant when employed as part of a mixture in a hanging basket, or as an individual trailing plant in a 13–18 cm (5–7 in) pot.

With a standard potting compost, a good light or some sun, and plenty of warmth in summer, it will quite happily flower. A cool season means no flowers until late mid-summer and it may then stop flowering in early autumn. It will drink a good deal at this time. Take off the flowers as soon as they have finished, unless you want seed; this will help to keep up the production of bloom.

When growth has finished for the season, cut off the trailing stems, back to where there will probably be new leaves and little shoots appearing. Keep it cool for the winter, and water sparingly. If you keep it too warm it will try to grow and weaken itself. Propagation is easy, by division in spring or by taking 5 cm (2 in) cuttings in late spring or early summer before flowers appear, and rooting them in warmth, shade and a peaty compost.

Capsicum**
Peppers 10–15°C (50–60°F). Tropics.

All sorts of peppers or capsicums have become popular in the last few years, either as vegetables, or as spicy flavourings for food. Strains of these have also been selected which are ornamental, bearing fruits that are particularly decorative. *Capsicum frutescens* and *C. annuum* are the two main parents; they are tropical plants mostly grown and used in India, Thailand, East and West Africa and Spain. Unfortunately the Christmas Pepper's exact country of origin is not known, as it has never been found in modern times growing in the wild, but it is on record as having been in cultivation since the middle of the sixteenth century. Sadly at that time no note was made of who discovered it, or where, though it is described in *Culpeper's Herbal*, published in the seventeenth century.

You will usually see them for sale during early to mid winter, with bright red, orange or yellow fruits, the colour depending on the stage of maturity. The fruit is long-cone-shaped, about 2·5 cm (1 in) long, held upright on a bushy little plant about 23 cm (9 in) tall, and if you make sure the atmosphere where the plant is growing is moist, the fruit will last a long time before they begin to wrinkle, and finally drop off.

They are edible, although because they have been selected primarily for their appearance, they will not be as well-flavoured as those grown for spicing food. However, they are very hot, so be warned.

Plants are raised from seed sown in gentle heat in the spring. Once the seedlings are of a reasonable size they should be potted into small pots of a loam-based mixture and gradually into larger ones as required. Syringe the leaves daily during the flowering period to assist fruit-setting. And give a dilute liquid feed at ten-day

LEFT:
Campanula isophylla (left) and C. i. 'Alba' (right) are delightful plants for containers which enable them to trail over the sides. The masses of charming flowers then cascade into space. It delights in a cool and draught-free place with plenty of air and light.

59

intervals when the fruits first appear and until they show colour.

In the summer they may be placed out of doors where they can have the protection of a sheltered wall.

Although the plants are often thrown away after fruiting, they can be kept and will flower and fruit again if given the right treatment. When the fruits have fallen, the plant can be rested by reducing the temperature and watering. Then, in early spring, cut last year's growth back by about half, repot the plant into fresh, fairly rich, compost, and give more warmth and water. Place outdoors in a sunny place once the danger of frost is unlikely, then flowers should appear in early summer. Bring in when the weather begins to get cold.

Watch for red spider mite, which are very partial to peppers, as are whitefly.

Chrysanthemum*
Hardy. China/Japan.

The chrysanthemum is a glorious flower which has a history of cultivation stretching back at least 2,000 years, though the modern types we grow are far removed from the early kinds. The type of chrysanthemum now sold all year round, as a bushy small plant, with a mass of flowers in the glowing autumn colours so typical of the chrysanthemum, has been given 'short-day' treatment to ensure that it will flower in succession through the year. It has also been watered with a chemical solution which has the effect of making it flower when small.

When you buy or are given one of these plants, it should flower for nearly two months. Look for a plant which has perhaps three or four blooms in flower and a mass of flower buds. If any of these have black centres, don't buy the plant; the buds should be green and quite near to flowering.

Water the plant daily, keep it cool and in a good light, and take off the flowers as they finish.

When flowering is over, if you continue to feed and water the plant, and cut the stems back a little, it will produce sideshoots, and the ones nearest the soil can be used as cuttings. These will produce normal-sized plants eventually, which flower in autumn or early winter. The parent plant is thrown away after flowering or being used for cuttings.

Cineraria cruenta* (syn. *Senecio cruentus*)
8°C (46°F). Canary Islands.
The florists' cinerarias have been selected during the last 60 years or so from a species of cineraria (syn. senecio) which inhabits the Canary Islands. The result is plants which are a mass of daisy-flowers, some single, some more or less double, in the most exquisite jewel-like colours. A display of the multiflora kinds in pots looks as though several rainbows at once have fallen on to the table. The royal blue and white kinds and the old rose-pink ones are especially distinctive.

You can buy pot specimens in winter, usually between early winter and spring. When growing them as pot plants, bought in flower, they will do best in a cool place, about 7–10°C (45–50°F). Give them plenty of water, as they drink a lot when in full flower, and lose a lot through their large leaves. A good light or a little shade, but never direct sun, is preferred, and a humid atmosphere.

It is best treated as an annual and discarded after it has passed its best. It is easily raised from seed sown at any time in the spring in cool conditions – an April sowing will, with luck, provide flowering plants for late December.

Citrus mitis**
Calamondin Orange 15°C (60°F). Philippines.
This neat little orange tree has only been easily obtainable from garden shops and stores since about 1965, but it has become very popular, in spite of its high price. To grow your own oranges in your own home is enough of an achievement, and miniature replicas are always fascinating, so a dwarf orange is bound to enchant and interest people.

The Calamondin Orange is one of the more choice potted plants, having many attractive qualities. Small glossy green leaves are attractive in themselves, and the plant retains a reasonably compact habit if the growing conditions are fairly cool, about 13°C (55°F). The white and heavily-scented flowers are mostly produced in the summer, but you may chance to have a crop of flowers at almost any time of the year for no apparent reason. Flowers are normally followed by small green fruits that will in time ripen to become perfect miniature oranges.

The fruits are 3·5 cm (1½ in) across, but are not sweet, rather sharp in fact. They make good marmalade.

The best method of cultivation is to pot the plant almost as soon as it is purchased if it is growing in a relatively small pot, which is usually the case. Two parts of loam-based mixture to one part peat will do them well.

New plants may be raised from seed or cuttings about 8 cm (3 in) in length – firm young shoots root fairly readily at any time of the year if a heated propagator is available.

ABOVE:
Cinerarias are indispensible for bringing colour to the home from December to April. When in flower give them plenty of water, allowing the surplus to drain easily away.

LEFT:
Citrus mitis, *the Calamondin Orange, is an unusual house-plant, in that it bears flowers and fruits at the same time. The flowers are white and highly scented, while the fruits – which are often inedible – are attractively coloured.*

OPPOSITE PAGE, LEFT:
Capsicum annuum, *one of the peppers, produces attractive red fruits. The plants can be raised from seed sown in gentle heat in the spring, and the seedlings when large enough potted into small pots. When the plants are in flower, syringe them daily to help the fruits to set.*

OPPOSITE PAGE, RIGHT:
Chrysanthemums are available the year round, in a variety of colours. They last a long time, especially during the winter months, and therefore are excellent as gift plants.

Clarkia*
Hardy. California.
Clarkia is another cheap and very cheerful annual that, if seed is sown in September, will provide attractive pot plants for the spring of the following year. Plants should be grown in cool conditions, transferring them to gradually larger size pots as the need arises.

There should be good light, as plants that are grown too hot, or in poor light, will become long and leggy, so much less attractive as pot plants. There is a wide range of colours available, separate or mixed and borne in dense spikes. Discard the plants after flowering.

Cyclamen persicum**
10–15°C (50–60°F). Syria.
Cyclamen are among the most popular, albeit difficult plants for winter flowering. They have attractive dark green rounded leaves, marbled with white or silver, and the pink, mauve, crimson or white flowers are carried high above the foliage.

They are very much better in a room or entrance hall where the conditions are light, airy and, above all, not excessively hot. Much is said, and often rightly so, about the danger of placing plants in positions where they are likely to be in a cold draught, but it is seldom that a cyclamen objects to windows being opened when weather permits. In moderately cool rooms plants will remain in flower for very much longer and will have a generally more healthy look about them than they do when exposed to hot, airless conditions.

Water cyclamen by standing the pot in water to avoid pouring water in among the leaves. Allow the soil to dry a little between each watering. Water remaining on the surface may cause rotting of the corm with subsequent rapid death.

When the flowers are over and the foliage turns yellow, cyclamen can be put out of doors and pots placed on their sides so that the soil drys out. When new growth is noticed in the centre of the corm the old soil should be completely removed and the plant potted up freshly, and watering, and feeding restarted. Cyclamen are difficult to keep growing from year to year, but it is worth trying.

Propagation is by seed, which germinates quite readily in a little heat and humidity.

Euphorbia pulcherrima**
Poinsettia 15°C (60°F). Mexico.
Whereas most of the winter-flowering plants require cool and airy conditions indoors to maintain them in good condition, the poinsettia is the exception to the rule and must have reasonable warmth if it is to prosper. Although excessive temperatures are not required, it is important that the minimum should not fall much below that recommended above for any length of time.

The growing position must be the lightest possible, and full winter sun will not present any problems, although if the plant is kept after flowering it should be shaded from strong sunlight in summer.

The bright green leaves are surmounted by large brightly coloured flower bracts. Bright red or scarlet is the usual colour, but pink and white forms are also available.

However, in spite of its need for more preferential treatment, the modern poinsettia is a very much more durable plant than its predecessors of two decades ago. In those days the varieties that were grown needed constant attention and a steady temperature if their leaves were not to shower off. The modern plants are not only very much more attractive as pot plants, they are also very much easier to care for both in the home and in the greenhouse.

Careful watering is reasonably critical, and one must use a programme that permits the mixture to dry out between each watering, so that the soil is kept just moist; over-watering and badly drained soil will cause the leaves to lose their colour and eventually fall off. How to get plants to flower again for a second time has become an almost standard question when poinsettias are under discussion – many indoor plant growers can get them to grow perfectly well for a second and third year in their homes, but no flowers will appear.

To encourage flowering the simple answer is that the plant from mid-September onwards should not be exposed to artificial light in the evening, as additional lighting simply results in the plant producing more and more leaves at the expense of flowers, or bracts. Even a street light outside the window of the room in which the plant is growing will prevent it from flowering. A weekly dilute feed during the summer months should also encourage new flower production.

FAR LEFT:
Of all the best known Christmas plants, perhaps the cyclamen is the first that comes to mind. Its stateliness of flower and leaf are instantly eye-catching, and this combined with its ability to produce flowers over a long period make it a must for most homes.

BELOW:
The Poinsettia, Euphorbia pulcherrima, is a difficult plant to grow in most homes. It needs a warm atmosphere, free from draughts, and good light. Nevertheless, it is a spectacular plant, with red bracts that often resemble flowers.

RIGHT:
Exacum affine is a most distinctive member of the gentian family. Plants become covered with wax-like purplish flowers, which last for a long time. It thrives in a steady temperature in a well illuminated room. However, too much strong light and sunshine will make the edges of the leaves turn brown.

BELOW:
Fuchsias were very fashionable in Victorian times, and then went out of fashion. Happily, they are again firm favourites in the gardening world and make superb flowering houseplants. This exciting variety is 'Snowcap'.

Exacum affine*

13–16°C (55–61°F). South East Asia.

Exacum affine is a flowering plant that seldom attains a height of more than 23 cm (9 in), and has bluish-lilac flowers that are pleasantly fragrant. The small, glossy green leaves are in themselves attractive. Grows best in cool and light conditions, and requires regular watering and feeding. Although they are perennial plants it is better to raise new plants each year.

These delightful plants can be propagated from seed by sowing it in late winter to early spring in a temperature of 18–20°C (64–70°F). Use a fine sandy compost, and prick the seedlings out when large enough to handle into 5 cm (2 in) pots of standard potting compost and then, as they grow, into larger pots as required.

Keep them in a humid atmosphere while being grown like this. Flowering should start in mid summer if sown in late winter.

Fuchsia*

4°C (39°F). Central and South America/New Zealand.

Fuchsias were very fashionable in Victorian times and then went out of fashion. They are now back in and it is difficult to see why they ever ceased to be popular.

Any specialist fuchsia catalogue will have a list of hundreds of hybrids; a few outstanding ones are: 'Ballet Girl', red and white, double; 'Flying Cloud', creamy white, double; 'Gruss an Bodethal', crimson and dark purple, single, small flowered; 'Mme Cornelissen', bright red and white, single; 'Marine Glow', white and deep purple, single; and 'Sea-shells', bright pink and shell-pink, double.

Fuchsias need to be kept on the cool side, with a little shade, and a good deal of humidity in hot weather. In summer, they like a daily spray with clear water, wetting the bark as well as the leaves. The temperature in winter should not drop below about 4°C (39°F) for the double-flowered kinds, but the small singles are more or less immune to frost.

If grown in containers in the home, fuchsias should be encouraged to rest in winter by putting them in a cool place and giving them little water, only just enough to keep the soil moist. In late winter, the previous year's growth can be cut back by half, or the whole plant may be cut harder. New shoots will appear very quickly once watering is increased and the temperature raised.

The compost used can be the standard potting mixture, repotting every spring or, if large plants, top-dressing only.

Fuchsias grow rapidly and can be kept bushy by taking out the tips of the new shoots, to leave three pairs of leaves on a shoot. Do not do this later than the end of spring, however, as flowering will be delayed by about ten weeks after the tipping. If all the sideshoots are removed, to leave one central stem, this will grow several metres (yards) tall, so that it forms

a standard; it will need a cane for support. The leading shoot should be stopped at the height required.

Flowerbuds and flowers drop if the compost becomes dry, if the atmosphere is dry, if there is too much light, or if the plant is moved when it is in flower. Troubles are few, but watch for red spider mite and whitefly, which often infest the plants, producing withered leaves which fall, or curling ones which gradually turn yellow and may develop sooty mould.

Gloxinia**

13–18°C (55–64°F). Brazil.

The florists' gloxinia should be more accurately described as *Sinningia speciosa*, but few florists would recognize the plant by the latter name, so gloxinia it is. Very fine seed is thinly sown in warm conditions in the spring of the year for preference, but may be sown later to give a succession of flowering plants. A peaty mixture is needed and plants should be potted into slightly larger pots. Good light, but shaded from hot sun, and a moist compost mixture, is important and dead flowers should be regularly removed to prevent them inducing leaves to rot.

As the plants develop, a tuber is formed from which leaves and flowers are produced. Give a weekly feed when buds appear. When the flowers and leaves naturally die down in the autumn, the mixture should be allowed to dry out, and the tuber, or corm, should be stored in a dry, warm place until the following spring when it can be started into growth by placing in a box or pot filled with moist peat. A temperature of not less than 20°C (70°F) should be maintained until growth is established. Green leaves that are large, velvety and very brittle should be handled with the greatest possible care. Many named varieties are available, all with clusters of trumpet-shaped flowers in shades of red, purple, pink and white, single or double and some with frilled edges.

Gloxinias are increased by leaf cuttings, in the same way as large leafed begonias.

Hibiscus**

Rose Mallow 7–16°C (45–61°F). South East Asia.

Most varieties of hibiscus have green leaves, although a few are variegated. The flowers of many hibiscus varieties are quite breathtaking, and come in many shades of yellow, red and orange in both single and double forms. In most instances the flowers of these shrubby hibiscus last for up to one week, depending on conditions. But the short life of individual flowers should not deter you from acquiring these plants, as there is a continual succession of flowers on healthy, vigorous plants.

To keep plants in good order they require lots of water during the spring and summer months, with a little less in winter.

In winter the mixture may be allowed to dry out so that plants shed their leaves and remain dormant until watering begins in the early spring; at the higher temperature the plants will retain their leaves. A light position and regular feeding are essential, and when potting plants into final containers it is best to use a peat-based mixture.

Plants are increased by taking cuttings about 10 cm (4 in) in length and inserting them in a peat and sand mixture in a warm propagator. Plants develop into bushes 1·8 m (6 ft) in height when grown in larger containers, but may be kept in check by regular pruning, which is best done in spring as growth restarts.

BELOW, LEFT:
Gloxinias are stately-looking plants, with large velvety and very brittle leaves — so handle them gently. Many different varieties are available, all with clusters of attractive trumpet-shaped flowers in shades of purple, red, pink and white, in single or double forms.

BELOW:
Hibiscus, the Rose Mallow, comes from south-east Asia, and produces flowers quite stunning in appearance. Individual flowers often last only about a week, but a succession of blooms are produced, giving a splendid display.

Hydrangea*
Hardy. China/Japan.

When purchasing hydrangea plants for room decoration it is important that pre-wrapped plants are not selected. A seemingly innocent protective paper bag can conceal many ills, so it is wise to insist on seeing the actual plants, and not just the few flowers that are showing at the top of the wrapping. With hydrangeas, a good buy is a plant no more than 60 cm (2 ft) tall, having stems well furnished with rich green leaves and at least five flower heads, some open with others follow. It should also be in a pot of not less than 13 cm (5 in) in diameter – there is seldom sufficient goodness in smaller pots to maintain hydrangea plants for any reasonable length of time.

Colouring of hydrangea flowers is also very variable so one should seek out those with a blue, pink or white colouring that is bright and well defined.

Indoors, the principal requirement of the hydrangea plant is a light and cool position in which to grow and an abundant supply of moisture at its roots while in active growth– during the winter the plant can be allowed to dry out completely. Whether plants are needed for growing or for producing cuttings in the spring, they should be placed out of doors during the winter and will benefit if they can have the protection of a glass frame.

In early spring they should be taken indoors again and watering should be started. Once a reasonable amount of growth has developed, plants can be potted into larger containers using a loam-based mixture, lime free for blue-flowered forms to maintain the colour.

New growth will quickly develop, and when it is obvious which of the shoots are going to produce flowers, select those that are blind for taking cuttings from to make new plants for the following year.

Cuttings root reasonably easily in a warm propagator in a peat and sand mixture.

Besides being fine room, conservatory and terrace plants, the hydrangea bought for room decoration may, when finished flowering indoors, be planted out in the garden.

LEFT AND BELOW:
Hydrangeas are stately plants with large heads of attractive flowers in late winter and early spring, and often continue until June or early July. Hydrangeas were first introduced from Japan in 1790 as a garden shrub, and have since been developed for both the garden and home.

Impatiens*

Busy Lizzie 10–13°C (50–55°F). Tropical Africa.

Known to everyone, Busy Lizzies propagate like weeds either in water or more conventionally in pots of potting mixture. Once the cuttings have rooted their tops should be pinched out to provide more bushy plants. Thereafter, pot on the plants as necessary and keep the peat- or loam-based soil most at all times. Feed the plants well when in their final pots.

Many excellent varieties are available to choose from, the colour range spanning white, pink, red, deep crimson, orange and purple. They flower almost continually and are all easy to grow in the pleasant warmth of a bright room that is well-ventilated on warmer days.

Causes of flower and flowerbud drop are draughts, dry atmosphere, dry compost, too much warmth, moving, and bright sunlight in summer.

This is a houseplant which is very easy to grow, and one well suited to novice gardeners. Children find these plants interesting.

Pachystachys lutea**

Lollipop Plant 15°C (60°F). Tropical South America.

This attractive plant produces curious upright cones of yellow-flowering bracts with protruding white flowers throughout the summer months and likes to be permanently moist and fed regularly. Pot on the plants when well rooted, into a loam-based mixture.

Cuttings of non-flowering shoots a few cm in length may be taken at any time if a warm propagating case is available. It is a plant that develops into a shrub of some 1·2 m (4 ft) in height, but can be kept under control by pruning after flowering. A light, warm position is needed indoors with shade from hot sun.

Passiflora caerulea**

Passion Flower. Almost hardy. Brazil.

Very vigorous plants *Passiflora caerulea* will need a framework of some kind for the tendrils to cling to as the plant develops. The foliage is formed of five-lobed dull green leaves, which is not particularly attractive, but this is more than compensated for by the colourful flowers that were a religious symbol for Christian missionaries. They saw in the petals the ten apostles of the Crucifixion, in the five anthers the five wounds, in the three stigmas the nails, in the purple rays of the corolla the crown of thorns. In the tendrils they saw the cords and whips and the five-lobed leaves resembled the cruel hands of the persecutors.

If given a light and airy window position, a gritty, loamy soil and reasonable watering and light feeding these are fairly easy plants to care

for. When too large for indoors they may be planted against a sheltered wall in the garden. Outside, they only succeed in the South of England.

Pelargoniums*

Geraniums 2°C (36°F). South Africa.

Pelargoniums must have been grown in pots on most cottage windowsills during the last 150 years. They seem to be almost indestructible and will produce a flower cluster or two under the most difficult conditions. They are easy to propagate.

There are several different groups; the regals, which have large, single, open trumpet-shaped flowers; the zonals, whose leaves have a dark band or zone on the surface and whose flowers are small and produced in rounded clusters (geraniums); the miniature zonals, up to about 15 cm (6 in) tall; the scented-leaved; the coloured-leaved, and the ivy-leaved.

Flowering is throughout the summer, except for the regals, which bloom for about a month in late spring to early summer. All are easily grown, and there is a tremendous number of varieties and a great range of colours – all except blue, in fact.

There are specialist nurseries which sell nothing but pelargoniums and they are so attractive it is very easy to be bitten with the bug of collecting and growing pelargoniums only.

The scented-leaved pelargoniums are more often grown as houseplants, but they make particularly attractive plants for surfacing window-boxes especially if the small-growing ones like *P. fragrans*, known as the Nutmeg-scented Geranium, and its variegated form are chosen. *P. crispum* 'Variegatum' is a beautiful foliage plant even without its lemon scent and quilted leaves and should be in every garden. The flowers of all the scented-leaved sorts are insignificant.

All pelargoniums, despite suggestions to the contrary, do grow in a reasonably rich moist soil containing a high proportion of loam, with occasional feeding. Starved plants will flower more freely but not with the same good-sized blooms: it really is a case of striking a reasonable balance.

Clay pots seem to yield better plants than plastic ones. Supply as much heat and light as possible in summer, and forget humidity. Feeding should not be necessary, if they are repotted every spring; if given too much nutrient they become very juicy-stemmed and leafy, grow like mad, and do not flower. Do not over-water the plants.

BELOW:
Regal pelargoniums are grown more as indoor plants than the popular bedding 'geraniums', and they do make impressive pot plants, as this picture of 'Fanny Eden' shows, flowering for many months.

Saintpaulias are delightful and colourful little plants for decorating windowsills and small tables. There is an abundance of colours available. They do, however, need careful watering — water must not be allowed to fall on the foliage and the compost should be free-draining.

Primulas are some of the best known winter and early spring pot plants. Primula obconica produces magnificent clusters of flowers in shades of red, pink or white. These are plants that will require plenty of water when they are in flower, but allow surplus water to drain freely from the pot.

Primula*

10–13°C (50–55°F). China.

With the winter-flowering primulas the principal requirement for success is cool and airy conditions, and they will do better for being in good light. Damp conditions at their roots and a moist atmosphere surrounding plants will also be beneficial, as will a soil mix with a reasonably high proportion of peat — most kinds will do well in an equal mixture of loam-based mixture and peat. Often you will find that very large plants are being sold in relatively small pots with not enough soil to keep the plants healthy. Such large plants are best potted into larger containers as soon as they are acquired — you may then witness an improvement.

The principal species are *P. malacoides* and *P. obconica*, both with light green hairy leaves in a rosette shape. The flowers, on tall stems above the leaves, are in large clusters and come in a wide range of colours; many are highly fragrant. The plants are treated as annuals and usually discarded after flowering.

People with sensitive skin would be well advised not to purchase or handle *P. obconica*, as there is every chance that quite severe skin irritation will be the result. Rubber gloves can be worn to minimise any skin irritation, which may be especially bad if the foliage is wet.

New plants can be raised from small seeds, but it is often better to purchase small plants and to grow them on if only a modest number is required.

Saintpaulia**

African Violet 13°C (55°F). Central Africa.

The man who first set eyes on some scruffy little violet-like plants in what was Tanganyika could not possibly have realized what a startling discovery he had made. Countless millions of these delightful plants are produced by the commercial growers annually, and countless millions more are raised by almost everyone who has a windowsill.

The African Violet must be one of the most popular of flowering houseplants, but also one of the most exasperating. They flower like mad for one owner, yet with apparently the same conditions, they will not bloom at all for another, only producing magnificent leaves or fading rapidly away.

The numerous varieties are available in single- or double-flowered forms, the violet-shaped flowers ranging from white through shades of pink, red, purple and blue. Leaves are almost round in shape, light or dark green according to the variety, and are covered in fine hairs. There are also varieties with leaves that are cristated, or waved.

Leaves that are fresh, of good colour and generally sound will root with little bother in small pots filled with a peat and sand mixture. They can be rooted in water, but the soil mixture method is best. A small, heated propagating case will speed the rooting process, as will dusting the ends of the cuttings with a rooting powder. When little bunches of leaves have

formed at the base of the leaf stalk (don't poke about in the soil, they will come naturally in their own good time!), the plant should have all the mixture gently teased away and the young plantlets can then be gently separated and planted individually in shallow pans of peat and sand.

When of reasonable size, pot them individually in a loamless mixture, and keep them in the propagator until they have become established. Treated in this way plants of more attractive appearance will result — it will take longer to get plants of any size, but they will show off their flowers very much better.

Saintpaulias are best grown in a peat-based soil; they must have adequate light, and this will mean a light windowsill during the day (but shaded from sun scorch) and going underneath a light of some kind in the evening during winter. Placing plants on a bed of moist pebbles will help to provide the essential humidity and they should ideally be watered with tepid, rather than cold water. Keep water off leaves and flowers — it is usually best to stand the plant in a saucer of water and allow it to draw up all that is required.

Established plants will benefit from a feed with a balanced liquid fertilizer. But if plants produce lots of lush leaves and seem reluctant to flower it may help if the fertilizer normally used is changed to a high potash one. Use this at a weak dilution every week — rather than a heavy dose occasionally.

Salpiglossis**
10°C (50°F). Chile.
These are good examples of half-hardy garden annuals that may be put to excellent use as pot plants. Indoors, they require cool, light and airy conditions with a watering programme that is never neglected.

Salpiglossis, with brightly-coloured flowers, make fine feature plants up to 60 cm (2 ft) high in an entrance hall of a house.

Seed may be sown at any time between February and September, and if sowing is staggered over this period plants may be had in flower from July through to the following spring. When potting use a loam-based mixture.

Solanum capsicastrum**
Winter Cherry 10°C (50°F). Brazil.
With lovely bright red or orange fruits, *Solanum capsicastrum* is a very cheerful subject at Christmas. It is a plant that enjoys the maximum amount of light and fresh air.

In poor light, Winter Cherries will shed their berries quickly, so a light and airy windowsill is absolutely essential.

Raised from seed these plants should be potted into small pots of a loam-based mix before being transferred to sheltered outdoor conditions for the summer months. Bring them under cover, in the home or a greenhouse, when nights become colder.

Keep the plants moist at their roots through-

out the growing season and spray the plants with water regularly once the flowers appear in summer, to improve pollination and help berries to set.

New stock can be propagated from cuttings taken from the previous year's plants. However, it is usually better to treat them as annuals and dispose of them once their attraction has gone, and to raise new plants from seed annually in spring. Seed should be sown at a temperature of 20°C (70°F) in early spring.

ABOVE:
The salpiglossis is an excellent example of a half-hardy annual which can be put to good use as a pot plant for house decoration. They require a cool and light position, and the soil should never dry out. They are propagated from seed sown any time between February and September.

71

height of about 46 cm (18 in) and S. × 'Mauna Loa', a much more majestic plant with flowering stems that may attain a height of 90–120 cm (3–4 ft) in good specimens.

The species *S. wallisii* flowers in spring and again in autumn; it may even flower on and off during the summer, and S. × 'Mauna Loa' flowers in spring only but is very fragrant. The spathes gradually turn green in due course but then remain healthy for some time.

Both are long-lasting plants and should grow for many years without much trouble.

Flowering is more likely to occur if you keep the plants in reasonably high temperatures. Although the winter temperature can drop to 10°C (50°F), flowers will only be produced if the temperature is maintained at 13°C (55°F), preferably higher.

A good deal of atmospheric moisture is important, otherwise the leaves dry at the edges, and become infested with red spider mite; overhead spraying and sponging of the leaves are both welcome. In summer, while growing, water freely, and also feed occasionally. Repot every spring using a peaty compost, and a pot slightly on the small side.

Propagation is easy, by division at any time when the plants are not in flower, though summer is probably better than in winter.

Sparmannia africana**

House Lime, African Hemp 7°C (45°F). South Africa.

The House Lime is an evergreen, tall-growing plant with large, pale-green, hairy leaves and clusters of white fragrant flowers each centred with a powder-puff of red and yellow stamens, in late winter and spring. It comes from South Africa, where it grows into a tall shrub 3–6 m (10–20 ft) tall – in a pot it grows fast to 90–120 cm (3–4 ft) tall.

The lower leaves turn yellow and drop, often because of a shortage of nitrogen, due in turn to the fact that it has grown faster than expected and used up the available nutrient in the compost. Draughts can also produce leaf drop, as can a dry atmosphere or dryness at the roots.

Water freely in summer, moderately in winter. Feed weekly during the growing season, and supply some humidity, including overhead spraying in hot weather.

It is a plant that needs good light and a temperature no lower than 7°C (45°F) in winter, though not too hot in summer. The standard potting composts can be used, and the plants repotted in spring and sometimes also in early summer, depending on the rate of growth. Pruning can be done after flowering, as required to keep the plant under control. Tip cuttings will root rapidly in summer, even in water.

Spathiphyllum**

White Sails, Peace Lily 13°C (55°F). Tropical America.

There are two species of this plant generally available: *S. wallisii* growing to a maximum

Stephanotis**

Madagascar Jasmine 10–15°C (50–60°F). Madagascar.

As climbing plants with exquisitely scented white tubular flowers borne in clusters, *Stephanotis floribunda* stand supreme. Leaves are leathery and glossy green and, being a natural climber, it is important that adequate supports are provided for the twining stems of the plant to twist around.

In winter they should have a light position that is not too hot, and the loam-based potting mixture should be kept only just moist. During spring and summer much more water will be needed, but it is important that the mixture should be free draining to avoid root rot that will result in discoloration and eventual loss of leaves.

The leaves have a tendency to turn yellow rather easily; this may be due to using alkaline water, an alkaline compost, letting the roots get dry or waterlogged, or allowing the temperature to drop too low in winter. If flowers and flowerbuds drop, it will be because the plant was moved, the temperature went up and down, there were draughts, the compost became dry, or the atmosphere was not moist enough.

New plants may be raised from cuttings in a warm propagator in a peat and sand mixture, or they may be raised from seed. By cross pollination of flowers you may be able to encourage your own plants to produce seed – the seed pod resembles a large oval-shaped green fruit and should be left on the plant until it turns yellow and actually splits open. It is quite an exciting

experience to see the silk-like textured seed 'parachutes' slowly expand and eventually emerge from the seed pod.

Streptocarpus*
Cape Primrose 10°C (50°F). South Africa.
The Cape Primroses are very pretty flowering pot plants which are not grown anything like as much as their appearance and ease of cultivation warrants. Although commonly called a primrose, they are members of the *Gesneriaceae* family, which provides several ornamental flowering pot plants for home and greenhouse, such as the African Violet, the columnea, and the Gloxinia.

The flower is trumpet-shaped, about 3·5 cm (1½ in) long, in ones or twos on slender stems 10 cm (4 in) or so high; the leaves are in a rosette like those of a primrose, with the flowers growing from the middle.

In spite of the newcomers, the old variety, *S. × hybridus* 'Constant Nymph', is still a firm favourite with its attractive blue flowers that bloom freely from May to October or even later.

The oldest leaves will turn yellow every season, and should be removed. Increase is by leaf cuttings in the same way as that for begonia leaves, or by seed (which needs great care as it is very fine) sown in spring in a temperature of about 15°C (60°F), or by careful removal of new rosettes in spring.

In the home they require good light and reasonably cool conditions in which to grow. Neither watering nor feeding should be excessive. A loam-based mixture with a little additional peat should be used when potting.

Tibouchina***
Brazilian Spider Flower 10–15°C (50–60°F). Brazil.
Tibouchina semidecandra is an interesting evergreen shrubby climber that is worth trying in a conservatory, where it can be grown in pots of rich compost.

If the plant is kept in full light and watered and fed well during the summer, it should produce clusters of rich purple flowers, each bloom 10–12·5 cm (4–5 in) across.

Water sparingly during the winter and prune established plants in February.

Cacti, succulents and bromeliads

These plants come in such a variety of shapes and forms that it is surprising that more are not grown, for many adapt very well to conditions in the home—and cacti are one of the few kinds of houseplants that can be forgotten during the fortnight's summer holiday without coming to too much harm.

The main difference between cacti and other succulents is that the stem of a cactus is swollen and used to store water, while in other succulents it is the leaves that are swollen. Most cacti are desert kinds, but there are forest cacti, such as epiphyllums and schlumbergas, which normally grow in trees. These forest cacti have flattened not swollen stems.

On the whole, both cacti and other succulents are grown for their interesting shapes, though both have flowers that can be very beautiful, and some such as the schlumbergera (Christmas Cactus) are grown primarily for their flowers.

With the exception of the forest type, cacti can take as much heat and sun as they are likely to be exposed to, yet will stand winter temperatures as low as 4°C (40°F), provided the roots are kept fairly dry. During the summer, however, they need regular and generous watering, even though they can survive periods without it.

The epiphytic or forest cacti do not need such intense heat and sunshine, and may appreciate some shade. Unlike the desert cacti, which require a well-drained soil, forest cacti like a compost rich in humus.

Succulents other than cacti are grown for their interesting leaf shapes, though many have attractive flowers too. Some succulents have fascinating leaf forms, such as lithops or Living Stones, which look like pebbles until they sprout their daisy-like flowers.

There are many plants that we grow in our homes and gardens but don't immediately think of as succulents, such as kalanchoes, sedums and sempervivums (Houseleeks), yet they are all part of this large group.

Cacti and succulents can be grouped together in pans and bowls. They can either be set in their own pots, which are then placed in a larger container and the spaces between the pots filled with a peat and sand mixture, or re-planted into a well-drained compost in the container. By leaving the individual plants in their own pots it becomes possible to remove plants from collection if they become too large.

Many people believe that cacti and succulents will grow in pure sand, but this is quite wrong. A good compost such as John Innes Potting Compost No. 1 or 2 is quite satisfactory. If additional drainage is required, extra coarse sand can be added.

Bromeliads form another distinctive group of plants. In their native habitat they grow mainly in the branches of trees, though some live on the ground. Most form a rosette of strap-like leaves which converge to form a hollow tube that collects water. This leaf formation is nature's way of channelling rainwater down the leaves and into the collecting funnel for the plant to live on. Little water is absorbed by the roots.

As bromeliads do not have deep roots they are best grown in pans — or several bromeliads can be grown on a dead branch of a tree or a piece of driftwood. They will need to be wired inconspicuously into suitable hollows and forks filled with a peaty compost. Sphagnum moss can be used to disguise any wiring.

Bromeliads should have the water in the funnel topped up every few weeks during the growing season, and a *weak* liquid feed can be introduced once a month while the plant is growing actively.

Aechmea*

Urn Plant 16°C (61°F) min. Central and South America.

The aechmeas (pronounced ek-me-a) are members of that curious but attractive plant family, the Bromeliaceae, and they have a very pronounced central funnel or vase. They are mostly epiphytes, that is, they grow on trees, though there are a few found growing on the ground, among rocks. They come from South America.

Aechmea rhodocyanea, (syn. *A. fasciata*, *Billbergia rhodocyanea*), is one of the most ornamental, as well as one of the easiest to grow, of the bromeliads. Its grey-green white-banded leaves and bright pink flower spike, covered in blue flowers, combine to make an extremely handsome and colourful, long-lasting houseplant. It comes from Rio de Janeiro and was first cultivated, in greenhouses, as long ago as 1826, but has only become really popular for home growing since about 1960.

The flowerhead lasts for several months, though each flower dies after a few days. The plant may be 60 cm (2 ft) high and at least 30 cm (1 ft) wide.

In winter, the temperature can drop to about 7°C (45°F); lower temperatures will result in varying degrees of leaf discoloration.

Aeonium*

7°C (45°F) min. Canary Islands/Azores/North Africa.

The aeoniums are succulents, members of the crassula family, and can be small or shrubby, or tree-like, with fleshy leaves either in rosettes at the end of shoots or flat and ground-hugging. The species are greatly varied in shape and colour; for instance *A. arboreum*, as it suggests, is like a miniature tree with brown branches bearing shiny green leaves and a main trunk to about 90 cm (3 ft) tall. Its variety *A. a.* 'Atropurpureum' has slightly smaller leaves, flushed with purple, which will keep the colour pro-

vided it is kept in bright sun and not in the shade.

A. tabulaeforme naturally grows pressed against rocks and is quite flat, the leaves being light green and tightly compacted. *A. undulatum* has rather spoon-shaped leaves with wavy margins, in rosettes on top of and around the main stem; it produces starry yellow flowers in clusters in summer. Height is 60–90 cm (2–3 ft); winter temperature should be 10°C (50°F), unless kept dry, though they tend to lose their leaves if kept too dry. A little water during the winter improves their appearance, as well as their health.

Agave*

5°C (41°F) min. Mexico.

The form of all agaves, which are succulents, is a rosette of fleshy, pointed leaves sitting close against the soil, from the centre of which is produced a flowering stem when the plant reaches maturity, sometimes at the age of 500!

Agaves are very attractive, and often form the centre-pieces of cacti and succulent collections, with smaller plants set around them.

The stem can be 7·8 m (25 ft) tall, as in *A. americana*, the Century Plant, whose spiny leaves can be 1·8 m (6 ft) long. In a container, however, it is very much smaller, growing only to about 1·2 m (4 ft), and is unlikely to flower. *A. victoriae-reginae* is more suitable for the home, slowly growing to 50 cm (20 in) wide, and 15 cm (6 in) high, with white-edged dull green, very fleshy leaves. It needs a minimum winter temperature of 10°C (50°F).

Agaves need more water than most succulents in summer, but need to be sparingly watered in winter.

75

Aloe*

5°C (41°F) min. South Africa.

The Partridge-breasted Aloe, *A. variegata*, is the most popular of the many species in this genus of succulents. It has a dark green rosette of leaves arranged in overlapping ranks, variegated with white horizontal bands. It is very handsome, about 10 cm (4 in) wide, and with light red flowers in a loose spike 30 cm (1 ft) tall in early spring. It does best if kept on the dry side in winter.

Ananas**

Pineapple 15°C (60°F) min. Tropical America. Although it seems highly unlikely, it is quite possible to grow *Ananas comosus*, the pineapple, in a dwarf form, in the home. It is a bromeliad, with narrow, spiny-edged green leaves in the usual rosette. There is a more interesting variety called 'Variegatus' whose leaves have a bright yellow margin. The variegated form is allergic to draughts.

The pineapple plants grown to produce fruit are about 2 m (6½ ft) in diameter, with 1·2 m (4 ft) long leaves, but there are dwarf forms for decorative use.

The pineapple is a native of tropical America, first introduced in 1690, and the fruit was given its common name because it was thought to look a little like the cones of the Scots pine which were then called 'pynappels'.

It makes an attractive foliage houseplant, but needs warm greenhouse conditions with a temperature of 33°C (90°F) to produce edible fruit.

Repot in spring and feed while the plant is growing. Increase is by detaching the offsets, or rooting the tuft of leaves at the top of the fruit in sandy compost, with warmth. As soon as the fruit is picked, slice the tuft off with one layer of pips, bury the layer in the compost, and put a plastic bag over pot and leaves until rooted.

Aporocactus flagelliformis**

Rat's Tail Cactus 5°C (41°F). Peru.

Aporocactus flagelliformis has long, glossy, green stems that later become grey, resembling rats' tails. This gives rise to its popular name.

The spines are reddish, later becoming brown. It has very lovely, colourful, profuse flowers, some 75 mm (3 in) long, emerging from the stems. There are a number of hybrids that produce flowers in a range of colours and in abundance. A beautiful one of these is *A. flagelliformis* 'Vulkan', which has scarlet flowers. An epiphytic plant, it requires rich soil and adequate watering.

Astrophytum***

Bishop's Cap Cactus or Star or Sea-urchin Cactus 5°C (41°F) min. Mexico.

The easiest of these to grow is the Bishop's Cap Cactus, *A. myriostigma*, with five very pronounced ribs forming a roughly circular body when young, covered with white scales and topped by small yellow fragrant flowers in

summer. *A. asterias* is the Star or Sea-urchin Cactus, a flattened ball with eight ribs and pale yellow, 2·5 cm (1 in) wide, flowers. It grows to about 10 cm (4 in) wide and 4 cm (1½ in) high in pots, but specimens growing in the wild can be 20 cm (8 in) and more in diameter.

Astrophytums can be grown in the usual cactus potting mix and under normal cactus conditions.

Billbergia*

Queen's Tears 15°C (60°F) min. South America. This bromeliad was named after J. G. Billberg, a Swedish botanist of the late 19th century. *B. nutans* is a terrestrial bromeliad, very easy to grow and will tolerate short spells of quite low temperatures. It produces rosettes of narrow serrated leaves, dark green, with great speed. A fully grown rosette is about 45 cm (1½ ft) tall. The unusual flowers hang in a graceful cluster from rose-pink bracts, and are coloured navy blue, green, yellow and pink. The flowering season is May and June, though they can be made to flower in winter if high temperatures can be provided.

Cephalocereus**
Old Man Cactus 5 °C (41 °F). Mexico.
The Old Man Cactus, *C. senilis*, is well named, as it is a column-shaped plant covered in long white hair, and looks more like some species of animal than a plant. On a good plant the individual hairs can be 13 cm (5 in) long. Plants can live to be very old – the 12 m (40 ft) specimens found growing in Mexico are estimated to be 200 years old. Unfortunately it does not flower until 6 m (20 ft) tall, and is extremely slow-growing, so when grown as an indoor plant, its chief attraction will be its hairiness. Some owners have been known to shampoo the hairs, to keep them a good light colour, but as the change from a clean creamy white to a rather dull beige is due to age, this is not very effective. It should be kept completely dry in winter.

Ceropegia*
Hearts Entangled 7°C (45°F) min. Natal.
It is difficult to believe that this genus is classed as a succulent. *C. woodii* belongs to the same family as *Hoya carnosa*, and has purple, long, hanging, thread-like stems, to 90 cm (3 ft), with small heart-shaped, fleshy leaves marbled white on green. From the axils of these grow greenish-white tubular flowers in summer. It grows from a tuber, and in winter can be kept quite cool and dry. The leaves will be fleshier the drier it is kept.

Chamaecereus*
Peanut Cactus 2°C (36°F) min. Argentina.
Chamaecereus silvestrii is a very easily grown and commonly seen cactus, with finger-like curving stems 3–8 cm (1–3 in) long lying flat on the soil, produced embarrassingly freely. These are easily knocked off or can be taken off and will root readily without any particular treatment, beyond making sure that the base is firmly in contact with the soil mix.

Bright red, open flowers about 2·5 cm (1 in) in diameter come in May, sitting directly on the stems. They will not set seed, however, because all the plants grown in cultivation have been vegetatively propagated.

In winter the temperature can drop to freezing and, provided it is dry, it will not be harmed, although it may shrivel a little, and will actually flower better.

Cleistocactus**
7°C (45°F) min. South America.
The name of this genus of cacti refers to the flowers; *cleisto* means closed and the flowers consist of a narrow, colourful tube, which never actually opens, though the stamens emerge from the end. *C. stransii* has erect columnar branches from the base, covered thickly with short white, rather prickly, spines, especially on the top of the column, which almost seems to have a top-knot.

Flowers only appear on well-established plants about 1·5 m (5 ft) tall and are red; they come continuously all through the summer,

from the sides of the plant. Offsets are readily produced. During the winter keep the soil mix just moist, not completely dry, unless the temperature goes down to freezing, and give them a slightly richer mixture than the usual.

Conophytum*
Living Stones 13°C (55°F). West and South Africa.
There are several kinds of succulent plants which have the common name 'living stone' (see also *Lithops*) because they are virtually indistinguishable, out of flower, from the pebbles, rocks and stones among which they live. Conophytums scrape a living from almost completely bare rock, where they grow in clumps. They are fascinating succulents that always arouse plenty of interest. They have the merit of holding interest both in and out of flower.

The seasons for resting and growing vary according to species; when they are resting, no water is given at all – they must be completely dry for the whole period.

Conophytum ficiforme has pink-lilac flowers 2·5 cm (1 in) wide which open at night, between autumn and spring. While flowering, it needs to be sparingly watered and given a good light and a temperature no lower than 13°C (55°F). At the same time as the flowers appear, new growth will also come and watering should continue until some time in spring when the plants begin to look dull coloured and have ceased to grow. Then they must rest completely, while the skin shrivels, for the summer months, in as hot and sunny a place as possible, until they start to look 'alive' again.

There is a selection of species available with flowers varying in colour – yellow, orange, purple, magenta or pink. They flower at different times, sometimes even in summer, so all must be treated individually as regards resting and growing.

RIGHT:
Chamaecereus silvestrii is commonly known as the Peanut Cactus. The numerous vermilion bell-shaped erect flowers are delightful, with golden anthers poised on reddish filaments. During its growing season it requires light, warmth and water, but in winter requires only a light and dry atmosphere, with little heat.

FAR RIGHT:
The Earth Star, Cryptanthus zonatus, is a fascinating plant that changes colour noticeably depending on the amount of light it receives. The specimen illustrated on this page has been grown in shade, the plant on the following page was subjected to strong light.

The conophytums increase naturally, forming larger and larger clumps. Individual plant bodies can be detached, with the stem, the skin removed, and then put into the standard well-drained compost for succulents, into which they will root.

Crassula*
7°C (45°F) min. South Africa.
The crassula genus is a large and varied group of succulents, containing shrubs and herbaceous plants.

Crassula arborescens is often seen as a pot plant not doing as well as it might, because it hasn't been watered. It is a small bushy plant, slowly growing to 90–120 cm (3–4 ft) after many years, with thick, spoon-shaped shiny leaves, and clusters of white starry flowers in late spring and early summer. *C. lycopodioides* is another commonly grown species, with small leaves pressed flat against the stems in layers, so that it looks like a collection of small green snakes.

Crassula falcata is a really beautiful succulent with thick, silvery grey leaves, shaped like sickles, and clusters of tiny red flowers on short stems in late spring; it is sometimes called the South African alpine rose. As it is inclined to lie down and turn into a prostrate plant, a support is a good idea. *C. lactea* has dark green, fleshy leaves and a cluster of fragrant white flowers on 15 cm (6 in) stems in late winter.

The crassulas are easily grown, provided you give them the water they need; without it the leaves gradually shrivel and fall off, the flowering kinds never do bloom, and the plants die slowly after a miserable existence. They need normal watering while flowering, and during the growing time that follows, but from then until mid or late winter very little is needed — just enough to keep the compost barely moist. Give them perhaps one watering a month if the temperature is about 4–9°C (39–49°F), but every two or three weeks if about 10–15°C (50–60°F).

If, after the resting period, the compost is very dry, the addition of 5 ml of liquid detergent to 4·5 litres (1 teaspoon to 1 gallon) of the water used for watering will help it to penetrate all the way through.

Do not worry about humidity for these plants. Put most species in as sunny a position as possible, though some become tinted red or brown in too much light, and feed once a month while growing. Repot every two years or so, just as they start to grow again; this may be spring or mid summer depending on the particular species.

Watch for mealy-bug, and root aphis, treat the former by brushing with methylated spirit, and the latter by repotting in fresh compost and watering with a solution of resmethrin. Do not forget to ensure that the pot is clean and free from bugs.

Crassulas are quite easily propagated by cuttings.

Cryptanthus*
Earth Star or Starfish Bromeliad 16°C (61°F) min. South America.
The cryptanthus are mostly rather flat growing, and the central vase is almost nonexistent. They are mainly terrestrials, though some grow on trees. They make good foliage houseplants, the flowers being insignificant, and because of their dwarf habit are also suitable for bottle gardens. The colouring of their leaves alters according to the intensity of light in which they are being grown; for instance *C. bivittatus minor* has two

ABOVE:
Conophytums — as with lithops — are commonly known as Living Stones, because they look like the pebbles amongst which they live. Conophytum pearsonii bears dainty daisy-like yellow flowers, and forms a bright display in many succulent collections.

cream-coloured longitudinal stripes on an olive green background but in strong light these stripes become flushed with deep pink. *C. fosterianus* (much larger, growing 45 cm (1½ ft) wide but only 8 cm (3 in) high) has succulent thick leaves banded horizontally with whitish-grey and copper brown in a good light, but when the light diminishes the leaves appear only dark and light green. *C. bromelioides* 'Tricolor' has light green leaves, broadly edged with cream, flushing to pink and is a little more upright than the other two, about 30 cm (1 ft) wide and high.

Use offsets to increase your collection of earth-stars. Although they produce flowers when growing naturally, the small flowerheads are the same colour as the leaves, and do not emerge from the centre of the plant.

Echeveria*
5°C (41°F) min. Central and Southern North America.
All echeverias are rosette forming succulents, with a single flower stem coming from the centre of the rosette, usually in winter or spring. *E. elegans* forms rosettes of almost white, translucent green leaves on stems eventually 30 cm

(1 ft) tall, with pink flowers. *E. gibbiflora* is shrubby with blue-green leaves, up to 20 cm (8 in) long, in rosettes flushed with red or purple; red flowers in autumn. The variety *E. g. metallica* has pink-bronze leaves with a pink or red edge, and *E. g. cristata* has frilled leaf margins. *E. setosa* has a flat and silvery rosette, with red flowers throughout summer. Give these plants a richer potting mix than usual and keep cool. Give water all year, but keep it off the leaves.

Echinocactus*
Golden Barrel Cactus 5°C (41°F) min. Mexico.
A small genus of about nine species, echinocactus includes the Golden Barrel Cactus, *E. grusonii*, one of the easiest to grow, provided it has as much sun as possible. It is almost completely round, with numerous ribs, each densely set with bright yellow spines. On top is a tuft of yellow wool-like hair. The flowers, which are rarely produced in cultivation, occur in summer and are yellow tubes. It is slow to grow and takes many years to reach 15 cm (6 in), and will stand a drop in temperature at night, and also near freezing in winter.

Echinocereus*

5°C (41°F) min. Mexico/Southern United States. *Echinocereus pectinatus* is a cactus with beautiful pink, tube-shaped flowers, the tube opening out at the end, and the whole flower being about 7·5 cm (3 in) long. Flowering goes on intermittently for most of the summer, the flowers starting as small dark woolly buds. Each flower lasts about two days. The spectacular flowers on *E. blanckii* are magenta.

The cactus body is a semi-prostrate column, with many ribs covered with small white spines. The soil needs to be specially well drained. Echinocereus are slow to grow, but produce offsets at the rate of about four or five to a plant. They can be kept quite dry all winter and will even take temperatures at frost level.

Echinopsis*

2°C (36°F) min. Argentina.
A very easily grown and flowered group of cacti, the echinopsis are small and round, flowering when about 7·5 cm (3 in) in diameter, the flowers being almost larger than the plants. *E. eyriesii* has fragrant, long funnel-shaped white flowers in summer; they open late in the day, and last through the next day.

Echinopsis have been in cultivation for a long time, and most plants are hybrids, crossed with lobivias, with freely-produced flowers in shades of pink, salmon, orange and yellow. Offsets are produced readily and are easily rooted when still tiny, about 1–1½ cm (½–¾ in) wide. No water is needed in winter, and they do not need much heat either. These delightful plants are so easy to grow that no collection should be without them.

Epiphyllum*

Orchid or Water-lily Cactus 10°C (50°F) min. Central and South America.
The epiphyllums have most beautiful flowers in late spring and early summer, and the recently produced hybrids have a second flush in the autumn as well.

The large flowers are gorgeous; they can be single or double, mostly in various shades of red, rose and pink, but also some white, orange and yellow. Stems must be two years old before they can flower, but thereafter flowers will be produced every year, though at different places on the stem each time. As well as being beautiful, some flowers are fragrant.

The stalkless flowerbuds are produced directly from the edges of the leaf-like stems (epiphyllum means 'on the leaf'), and start to develop two months or so before they actually

unfold. Each flower lasts three or four days.

Out of flower, epiphyllums are ungainly plants, with a tendency to droop awkwardly about the place. They usually need attaching firmly to supports.

In order to flower well, epiphyllums must have plenty of light, even some sun, though not the really hot midday sun of high summer. Small fat buds will start to appear on the stem edges in early or mid spring and will open in late spring. Don't move the plant at this time or when flowering; the buds develop facing the light, and moving or turning the plant will result in bud drop. Flowers may also drop for no apparent reason — it is usually nature's way of getting rid of too many.

There are many hybrids. Some good ones are: the E. × ackermannii range, which includes all the red hybrids, and E. cooperi range, with the snow-white and yellow hybrids, fragrant and opening in the evening; 'London Sunshine', yellow; 'Midnight', purple and pink; 'Sunburst', salmon with red centre; 'Wanderlust', dark pink.

A standard potting compost with extra peat and good drainage is preferred, as are pans rather than pots, for their shallow roots. A 13 cm (5 in) size will do for one plant, and don't forget the supports, otherwise you'll have an overbalancing plant. Repotting is done after the first flowering of the season, at the end of the rest.

Plants are increased from cuttings: use the tip of a new shoot, in early summer, and cut it off at a convenient joint so that the cutting is about two or three joints long. Let the cutting dry for about three days — the end will callous — and then put it about 2·5 cm (1 in) deep in moist coarse sand, with a little support, and cover with a plastic bag, for quicker rooting. Warmth helps as well.

The resting period of epiphyllums is mainly winter, after the second flush, but they also have a short resting time in early summer, after the first flush of flowers.

Euphorbia*/**
10°C (50°F) min. Madagascar.

This genus is very large and extremely varied in its forms, from succulents through annual and perennial herbaceous plants to shrubs and trees. The sap is white and milky. The ferociously prickly spines of E. milii (Crown of Thorns) are rather off-putting, though the red flowers dotted all over it in spring and the fresh, light green leaves are pretty enough to make up. The grey stems are thick, fleshy and gnarled, to 1·2 m (4 ft). Its resting time is winter. It needs to be kept slightly warmer and moister than other succulents, with some water throughout the entire year.

Faucaria**
Tiger's Jaws Cactus 5°C (41°F) min. South Africa.

The leaves of these are tough and fleshy. F. tigrina (Tiger's Jaws) are armed with teeth along the edges, and their grey-green colour sets off the bright yellow flowers produced in autumn — they open in the afternoons. The plant is only about 7·5 cm (3 in) high.

Keep faucarias in small pots to encourage flowering, and keep dry in the early spring and summer.

BELOW:
Most people will have heard of the Crown of Thorns plant, which botanically is Euphorbia milii (E. splendens). It is characterized by its long and sharp thorns, making the whole plant in need of careful handling. Its bright scarlet flower-like bracts, which are borne in pairs, make it an attractive plant.

Fenestraria**

Window Plants 2°C (35°F) min. South Africa. Sometimes this succulent is sold or listed under the name mesembryanthemum, but it is quite different to those plants in its habit of growth, and looks very much more like Living Stones. Fenestrarias have attained their common name because the surface of each swollen pebble-like leaf is transparent. This allows just enough sun to reach the plant for it to live — the rest of it being buried — but not so much that it is burnt up. *F. rhopalophylla* forms clumps of cylindrical greenish-white leaves and has white flowers 3 cm (1½ in) wide; the species, *F. aurantiaca* is similar but with yellow flowers.

Plenty of sun, a wide shallow container and a little water throughout the year are advisable.

Ferocactus**

5°C (41°F) min. Central America/Southern United States.

Fero means ferocious, and this describes the spines of these cacti exactly. They are long, stout and exceedingly pointed, and some are hooked as well. These cacti are grown for their spines, as flowers are rarely produced. The plant body is round and ribbed until the adult stage when it becomes more or less columnar. It slowly grows to a diameter of about 37 cm (15 in) in the species *F. latispinus*, whose small, red and scented flowers may be produced in late spring and summer on top of the plant. Some species can be 3 m (9 ft) tall. *F. melocactiformis* has yellow spines and flowers in June and July, and grows to about 60 cm (2 ft). Give as much sun as possible, and let the plants dry out between waterings in summer.

Guzmania*

16°C (60°F) min. Central and South America. The guzmania cacti have become popular as houseplants over the last 10 to 15 years, since hybrids have been widely introduced. The flowerhead is spearheaded in shape, though in some species it gradually opens out later into an almost waterlily-like shape. Apart from their rosette habit, guzmanias vary considerably in colouring, flower and leaf, but all are handsome. *G. lingulata*, which grows to 30 cm (1 ft) high, has a brilliant red flowerhead, and small white flowers surrounded with orange to yellow smaller bracts. *G. zahnii* has olive green leaves striped with red, red bracts on the flower stem, and a yellow flowerhead with white flowers; height is about 60 cm (2 ft). *G. berteroniana* has a brilliant red flowerhead and yellow flowers; leaves are light green or wine red, and height is about 45 cm (1½ ft). All guzmanias flower in the winter, and nearly all are epiphytes.

Gymnocalycium*

5°C (41°F) min. Northern South America. You sometimes see, at shows and in nurseries, some extraordinary-looking cacti with bright red scarlet balls on top of fleshy green columns. The red ball is the gymnocalycium which has been grafted on to a stock of *Myrtillocactus* or *Trichocereus*. This red gymnocalycium is a cultivar called 'Red Ball' from *G. mihanovichii friedrichii*; as it does not contain any chlorophyll, it has to be grafted to grow at all. The plant is cultivated because of its red colour and is unlikely to flower. There is also a yellow form and a red and green striped one.

The ordinary gymnocalyciums are mostly round plants about 5–15 cm (2–6 in) in diameter with a few ribs and spines of varying size. Large flowers come from late spring through June and July; they last for four or five days, and are often bigger than the plant. Colours are in shades of pink or red, but sometimes white and yellow are also seen. No special care is needed beyond the normal cactus cultivation.

Haworthia*

5°C (41°F) min. South Africa. These succulents of the lily family are small plants or shrublets, usually rosette-shaped. *H. margaritifera* has dark green, fleshy leaves, heavily marked with white, in a rosette up to 15 cm (6 in) wide. *H. reinwardtii* forms a tall narrow rosette of fleshy, keeled leaves, up to a height of 15 cm (6 in). Haworthias like a good light but not full sun and a little water in winter.

Kalanchoe*

5°C (41°F) min. South America/China/Madagascar.

Kalanchoe blossfeldiana 'Tom Thumb' is a small succulent with rounded fleshy leaves and clusters of small, bright red flowers, often for sale at Christmas; there is also a variety with yellow flowers.

The flowers last several weeks at least, and once finished should be removed together with their stems back to a pair of leaves.

Kalanchoes are 'short-day' plants, so the time of flowering can be manipulated by shortening the day length during spring and summer. After winter flowering has finished, give the plant less water until it starts to produce new shoots and leaves, then increase it and put the plant in as light a place as possible — in a garden is best of all — in early and mid summer. This will ripen the growth so that it flowers the following winter, but if you want flowers in mid to late autumn then cover the plant with black polythene so that it only receives 8½–10 hours of daylight during early and mid summer, and keep the temperature at about 16°C (60°F). Covering it earlier or later will vary the flowering time accordingly.

Kalanchoe tomentosa is quite different, with thick, furry, silvery leaves, edged with chocolate brown hair, and silvery stems, to 75 cm (2½ ft); a very handsome plant seldom producing flowers. Other kalanchoes include those formerly known as *Bryophyllum*; they produce plantlets on the edges of the leaves in between the serrations, which drop off and root easily into the soil below. *K. diagremontiana* has pointed leaves, flat and arrow-shaped, and marked with purple-brown. The winter flowers are yellow and pink, and it grows up to 60 cm (2 ft) tall. *K. fedtschenkoi* has blue-purple leaves fading to lilac-pink, with dark toothed edges, and yellow flowers in winter. Height is about 30 cm (1 ft). Kalanchoes are easily grown, needing slightly more water in summer and more food than most succulents; they also like humidity.

Lithops*

Living Stones 5°C (41°F) min. South Africa. These succulents are more like stones than any of the other mimicry succulents and the name is taken from the Greek *lithos*, stone, and *ops*, like. Sometimes also called pebble plants, they come from south and south-west Africa where they grow in desert conditions of sand, gravel and a little soil. There they are almost completely buried and the surface of the succulent leaves is the only part which shows above ground. As the

LEFT:
Kalenchoe blossfeldiana *is a floriferous succulent, reaching a height of about 22 cm (9 in). It is easy to grow, needing slightly more water in summer than winter.* Kalanchoe blossfeldiana *is available in several different varieties, one of the best being 'Tom Thumb'. 'Morning Star' and 'Vulcan' are two other good varieties.*

LEFT:
Lithops, often better known as Living Stones, look exactly like the pebbles among which they normally grow. Only the surface of the plant can be seen, the rest is buried from the hot desert sun. The daisy-like flowers appear in late summer and autumn. They require a well-drained compost.

surface is marked with patterns of grey, pink, brown, yellow or dull grey-green, they are effectively camouflaged from browsing animals.

Each plant consists of two extremely fleshy leaves, nearly completely joined, from the centre of which appear yellow or white daisy flowers in late summer and autumn. They rest between December and April, and need a potting mix consisting of almost half coarse sand or other drainage material. When they start to grow again, the dead outer skin will split, and each lobe bursts through it. Keep the plants dry while resting, and water only sparingly even when growing.

Growth is slow, and they rarely form clumps, so potting every two or three years is all that may be necessary, in mid to late spring. The plant body should be buried by about a quarter of its size.

Lobivia*

2°C (36°F) min. South America, particularly Peru.
The main attraction of these cacti is their flowers, which are large, up to 10 cm (4 in) across, and brightly coloured pink, red, purple, white, yellow or orange. They are funnel-shaped and occur in summer, and quite young plants of two or three years will flower; an added attraction is the ease with which they can be grown to flowering size. Although the flowers only last for a day, they come in quick succession and fresh buds are constantly appearing.
The plant body is small and round, 5–15 cm (2–6 in) in diameter. Some especially good species are *L. aurea*, bright golden flowers; *L. cinnabarina*, an almost luminous red; and *L. jajoiana*, deep red with a black throat. Lobivias will endure frost, if the roots are kept dry.

Mammillaria*

Pincushion Cacti 5°C (41°F) min. Central and South America/West Indies.

Whole books have been written about mammillarias, and there is an entire society for mammillaria enthusiasts. It is a vast genus of over 200 species, very varied in plant forms and with species whose care ranges from easy to very difficult. The small flowers are produced in a ring round the top of the plant, which can be globular or cylindrical; flowering starts in early summer and can continue until autumn. Sometimes brightly coloured fruits follow and last until the new flowers the following season. On the whole, they are small plants, growing to, at the most, 20 cm (8 in) tall, singly or in clusters. All have prominent spines, sometimes prickles, sometimes hair-like.

Some suitable species for a windowsill are: *M. wildii*, white flowers all through summer, clustered plant body; *M. zeilmanniana*, red-purple flowers on tiny plants, cylindrical but branching; *M. rhodantha*, red spines and magenta flowers in mid-summer, cylindrical; *M. microhelia*, golden spines and greenish yellow flowers, solitary body. *M. rhodantha* has a cristate or fasciated form, and so has *M. wildii*, which will also flower quite freely. Plenty of light is important for flower production, and the plants should be turned frequently to prevent them straining towards the source of light.

Neoregelia**

16°C (61°F) min. Brazil.

The shapes and forms of plants are everlastingly different and interesting, and even within the strange family of bromeliads, there are variations of the central funnel and the form of the flowerhead. The neoregelias come from the rain forests of Brazil, and the flowerhead is different from that of the other bromeliads in that it never really comes right out of the funnel. It forms a kind of rosette in the base, barely above the water, and the large, brightly coloured flowers pop out all over the top. Late spring and early summer are the times of flowering.

Probably because the flowers are low down and would be easily missed by pollinating insects, the centre of the funnel of most neoregelias is brightly coloured; if it is not, then the flowers, though small, are plentiful and brilliant.

Neoregelia carolinae 'Tricolor' is one of the most popular varieties, with outer green leaves centred with yellow or white, the inner ones pinkish-red; the flowerhead is bright red, with violet flowers, but it stays within the rosette and does not grow on a stem. Flowering is in late spring and summer; the flat rosettes can be 40 cm (16 in) wide. *N. concentrica* has broader leaves 10 cm (4 in) wide and 30 cm (1 ft) long; they are purple blotched. The bracts are purple and the blue flowers appear in the centre on a kind of pincushion.

Nidularium**

16°C (61°F) min. Brazil.

These epiphytic bromeliads are very like the neoregelias to look at, but their cultural treatment is different — they need more shade and humidity and higher temperatures to produce flowers. The name means a small nest, and refers to the flowerhead, which does not emerge from the rosette, but remains compact so that the flowers appear on a mound in the water in the vase. *N. innocentii* has dark red to almost purple-black leaves, and the tightly-packed flower bracts, in autumn, are orange to copper coloured with white flowers sitting on top; *paxianum* and *nana* are particularly attractive varieties of this. *N. fulgens* has white and violet flowers, and leaves spotted dark green.

Notocactus*

5°C (41°F) min. Central South America.

A large group of vigorous, easily-grown cacti, the notocactus are easy to flower, mainly small, growing up to 17 cm (7 in), and round with flattened tops and many spines on the ribbed sides. Trumpet-shaped flowers, opening out wide, are usually yellow and large for the size of the plant, coming either singly or in a circle from the top. *N. haselbergii* is covered in white spines, so that it looks like a white ball, and has orange red flowers in early summer lasting for several weeks, though it does not start to flower until about five years old. *N. leninghausii* grows up to 90 cm (3 ft), has yellow spines and yellow flowers in summer, but these do not come until it is a column about 17 cm (7 in) tall. *N. apricus* is a name covering a group of plants growing about 8 cm (3 in) high, whose flowers are large and yellow, appearing on even tiny plants; they have a dense covering of bristly brown and highly attractive yellow spines.

BELOW:
Neoregelias are epiphytic bromeliads from the rain forests of Brazil. However, because of the tough, water-resistant nature of their leaves they are able to withstand a dry atmosphere, often present in most homes. Neoregelia carolinae 'Tricolor' is one of the best known of these plants, with attractively coloured leaves.

Opuntia*

Prickly Pear 3°C (37°F) min. North, Central and South America.

The Prickly Pear cacti have taken to Australia and warmer parts of Europe so readily since their introduction that they have been thought to be indigenous. The fruits of the opuntia can be eaten, and are grown in some areas of America for canning. The best known opuntias are those with flattened pads, but there are also tree-like types with cylindrical, branching stems. The smaller species, with pads, are the easiest

to grow in the home. Opuntias are not difficult to grow, but flowers are rarely seen except under greenhouse conditions; the plants are usually grown for their shape and colourful spines with barbed bristles. These can become embedded in the skin and are difficult to remove.

Suitable species, flowering occasionally, include *Opuntia microdasys albispina*, a smallish, neat plant with pads, and pale-yellow flowers, if you look after it the right way. It is not prickly, but it does have tufts of white hairs, hooked at the ends, on the pads, so be careful handling it. If it gets cold, brown spots appear on the pads. *O. bergeriana* has dark-red flowers, and oval pads; it grows wild in the south of France but may be difficult to flower in the home without sufficient heat and sunlight. *O. basilaris* has red flowers and purple-blue pads, growing to 90 cm (3 ft); *O. microdasys* is yellow-brown and spineless with yellow flowers occasionally, growing 90 cm (3 ft) high. *O. paraguayensis* has yellow flowers and is the most easily flowered of this selection.

Parodia**

5°C (41°F) min. Central South America.

Globular cacti, small and slow growing to 6 cm ($2\frac{1}{4}$ in), the parodias' main attraction is their spines. *P. chrysacanthion* has long, pale yellow

LEFT, ABOVE:
The Prickly Pear group of cacti originated from North, Central and South America. Opuntias, as they are botanically called, are not difficult to grow, but normally only produce flowers under greenhouse conditions. Opuntia micro-dasys has yellow-brown spines and, occasionally, yellow flowers.

LEFT:
Parodia sanguiniflora is a delightful and spectacular little cacti, displaying brown spines and numerous dark red flowers in summer. Originating from Central South America it requires careful watering, especially during the winter months, as parodias rot quite quickly if their roots are continually in water.

The rebutias are marvellous cacti for flowering; they are small globular plants, maximum height 13 cm (5 in), producing many offsets. The trumpet-shaped flowers are produced near the base of the plants in great profusion, almost covering the plant in spring. Some species virtually flower themselves to death, but they are so easily rooted from offsets or grown from seed, that replacements are easy.

Flower colour can be yellow, red, lilac, salmon, pink, orange and white. The rounded plant is not ribbed and has very few spines. Rebutias need good light in summer, but virtually no heat or water in winter. Some especially good species are: R. minuscula, red flowers and one of the earliest to bloom; R. senilis, red flowered from April onwards with long white spines; and R. xanthocarpa salmonea, salmon-pink.

Rotting is usually caused by wet compost in winter, or too much warmth then. Red spider mite and mealy-bug should be watched for in summer.

Rhipsalidopsis**
Easter Cactus 13°C (55°F) min. Central and South America.
The Easter Cactus, R. gaertneri, was formerly known as Schlumbergera gaertneri, and before that as Zygocactus gaertneri and it may be sold under any of these names. The Easter Cactus is one of the hanging types of cactus, with flattened leaf-like stems about 1–1·5 cm ($\frac{1}{2}$–$\frac{3}{4}$ in) wide, segmented into dull green pads. New growth appears from the tips of the end pad, as do the flower buds. A well grown plant may be 45 cm (1$\frac{1}{2}$ ft) high and 45 cm (1$\frac{1}{2}$ ft) wide, and when in full flower is extremely attractive. The flowers are trumpet-shaped and pendent with narrow, pointed, red and purple petals, appearing in April and May, smaller but more numerous than those of the Christmas Cactus.

The Easter Cactus rests from autumn (September) to late winter, then begins to push out new flower buds; after flowering it grows new pads during summer, on which next year's flowers will come. Do not subject it to artificial light in the evenings in autumn and early winter, as this can influence the time of flowering.

Rochea**
7°C (45°F) min. South Africa.
The French botanist La Roche (d. 1813) is commemorated in the name of this succulent. The best known species is R. coccinea, a shrubby plant which grows to about 60 cm (2 ft) tall, with small fleshy leaves arranged in regular ranks up the stem, and a head of red fragrant flowers at the top from May or June onwards. R. jasminea has prostrate stems and white flowers in spring. Take off the dead flower stems to make room for new shoots, which will themselves flower later in the season. Rochea need water all year, and will benefit from a little shade in summer.

spines covering it, and sometimes small yellow funnel-shaped flowers. P. faustiana has white spines and brown flowers, P. sanguiniflora has brown spines and numerous dark red flowers in summer, and P. mairanana has yellow spines and apricot flowers from summer until autumn. Be careful with watering, particularly in winter, as parodias are extremely susceptible to their roots rotting.

Rebutia*
5°C (41°F) min. Mountains of South America. These readily flowering cacti were named after a French cactus grower, P. Rebut, who lived during the 19th century. They come from northern Argentina and Bolivia, and can be found growing as high up in the mountains as 3600 m (11,000 ft), almost straight out of the rocks. It is difficult to understand how they obtain any sustenance at all and yet they flower profusely and will even start to do so as one-year-old seedlings. Some rebutias will flower twice a year.

Though mammillarias are so popular, rebutias are even more so with specialist cactus growers, because of their ease of cultivation and floriferousness, so you can assume they will be a good plant for the home, in a sunny place.

Schlumbergera × buckleyi**

Christmas Cactus 13°C (55°F) min. Brazil.

If you see a plant for sale called *Zygocactus truncatus*, that is another name somctimes still used for the Christmas Cactus. Sometimes you will see one called *Schlumbergera gaertneri*, but this is not the same; it is another name for the Easter Cactus (see *Rhipsalidopsis*), which flowers much later.

Flowering can be between October and late January depending on variety and cultural care, but it will not form flowerbuds unless it is subjected to short days. The drooping, narrow trumpet-like flowers, up to 8 cm (3 in) long, are magenta or rose-pink. If you keep it in the house in the autumn and early winter, it must not be given artificial light when it is naturally dark outdoors; the plant must still be kept in warmth, but in a dark place in the evening.

Habit of growth and flowers are very much like the Easter Cactus, but the larger and fewer flowers are more easily produced. It rests from late winter until late spring, then starts growing again, and in September the flowerbuds should begin to appear. If you delay giving it short days, it will take longer to form buds, and once you are experienced, you can manipulate flower production so that it coincides with Christmas.

A temperature of about 18°C (64°F) also helps to encourage flowering.

While the plant is in flower, water it as you would an ordinary indoor plant, give it a good light and a temperature of about 13–18°C (55–64°F), and a humid atmosphere. Bud drop will occur if you move the plant, change the temperature or the light, keep the plant short of water or in a draught, or expose it to gas or a dry atmosphere. They are rather temperamental at this time!

When flowering has finished, decrease the watering considerably so as to keep the compost barely moist, but leave the plant in the same conditions otherwise. In late spring, it can go outdoors in a sheltered, slightly shaded place to be rained on. Raise it on bricks to help drainage. Too much light in summer makes the stems go red. During this time it will grow new stems or lengthen the old ones. In late summer and early autumn, keep it slightly on the dry side to help ripening.

Repotting is not required annually; once every third year or less often is sufficient, using a standard compost, with plenty of extra humus, and a sprinkling of bonemeal.

They are delightful plants, and many people manage to keep them for several years.

ABOVE:
One of the best known rocheas is R. coccinea, *an attractive shrubby plant with small fleshy leaves arranged in regular ranks up the stem and with a head of fragrant red flowers on top.*

Sedum*

5°C (41°F) min. Worldwide except Australia. This large genus also includes small succulent plants and there are many attractive species which grow well in the home. *S. sieboldii* 'Medio-variegatum' has fleshy blue-green leaves with a pale yellow or white stripe in the centre and red edges; in September it produces clusters of pink flowers, but then dies down completely for the winter. *S. pachyphyllum* (Jelly Beans) which grows to 30 cm (1 ft), has blue-green fleshy leaves, clubbed and red at the tips and red and yellow flowers in spring. *S. rubrotinctum* is a small plant of about 20 cm (8 in), and has small, thick, berry-like leaves which turn coppery red in the sun; the yellow flowers are seldom seen. Feeding is not required; shallow containers are best and keep the potting mix on the dry side.

Selenicereus**

10°C (50°F) min. West Indies.
Most of the species of this genus are night-flowering and are responsible for getting cacti in general a bad name for flowering once every seven years. *S. grandiflorus* (Queen of the Night) unfolds its beautiful blooms in the evening and they last all night, but they are produced much more frequently than every seven years. The white flowers are enormous, up to 30 cm (1 ft) long, and very strongly scented, produced in June or July. The trailing or climbing stems can be 5 m (17 ft) long in the wild, but in a container are less than half that length. The plant must have warmth in winter in order to produce buds.

Sempervivum*

Houseleek 2°C (36°F) min. Europe.
These succulents are so well known as to hardly need description. Cultivation is easy in the extreme, as they seem able to exist virtually without any water – an occasional deluge every few months is sufficient.

The Common Houseleek, *S. tectorum*, consists of rosettes 10 cm (4 in) wide of fleshy pointed triangular leaves. *S. arachnoideum* is the Cobweb Houseleek, with tiny rosettes 2·5 cm (1 in) wide covered in white webbing, from the centre of which come stems 7·5 cm (3 in) or more tall, carrying starry flowers in June.

Stapelia*

5°C (41°F) min. South and Tropical Africa.
Stapelias are unlucky to have a reputation for smelling unpleasant, because it is only a few species which do so; the rest have no odour of any kind. The whole plant is fleshy including the flowers, which have bizarre and spectacular colouring. *S. grandiflora* has starfish-shaped blooms 15 cm (6 in) wide, dark brown, with fringed and hairy petals. *S. revoluta* can reach a height of 37 cm (15 in) and has purple flowers; the flowers of *S. verrucosa* are saucer-shaped, yellow with red spots – it is a small plant. The most well known one, *S. variegata* grows to 10 cm (4 in), has pale yellow wrinkled petals with dark purple spots, but this is one of the evil-smelling species.

All flower in summer and rest in winter; they need an ordinary potting mix with extra grit. A larger pot than usual is required as they need plenty of root room, as well as a little shade from sun in summer.

Tillandsia**

16°C (61°F) min. West Indies/Central America. The variation in habit of this genus of bromiliads is very great – it comes from tropical rain forests as well as deserts and steppes, and there are therefore both terrestrial and epiphytic forms. The Spanish Moss is an epiphytic species of tillandsia, *T. usneoides*, and if you wish to grow this, a bromeliad tree is ideal, so that the long trails can hang down from the branches. *T. lindeniana* is the Blue Bromeliad; it has large, brilliantly blue flowers emerging from a flattened spike of deep rose-pink bracts on a stem about 30 cm (1 ft) long, and is altogether a very showy plant, flowering in summer. The leaves are narrow and pointed, dark green and purple.

Vriesea**

Flaming Sword 16°C (61°F) min. Central and South America (esp. Brazil).
The vrieseas are bromeliads, named after a Dutch botanist, W. H. de Vriese who lived during the last century. The Central and South American rain forests are the home of these striking and dramatic-looking plants whose flower-heads are coloured red, yellow, or red and yellow together. They are most handsome but, unlike the majority of bromeliads, they need more warmth and a good deal of humidity to do well.

One of the most commonly grown and attractive is *Vriesea splendens* (Flaming Sword), a bromeliad whose 50 cm (20 in) long leaves are cross-banded in dark brown-purple. The sword-shaped flowerhead is red with yellow flowers, and appears in mid to late summer; it will take about four years for a flower to appear from a detached offset, and this accounts for the high price of these plants. The flowerhead may last two months and the leaves will be attractive for long after that.

Another good species is *V. gigantea* (syn. *V. tessellata*) whose 45 cm (1½ ft) long leaves have a kind of snakeskin marking of yellow on the upper surface and red-purple beneath; the flower rarely appears in home cultivation. *V. psittacina* has shiny light-green leaves, and a red flowerhead in mid summer from which green-tipped flowers protrude.

Give these plants the normal bromeliad treatment as regards light, compost, food and potting, but do not let the winter temperature fall below 18°C (64°F). Keep them in a very humid atmosphere, and water moderately in summer with tepid soft water, but in winter, empty most of the water from the 'vase' and thereafter give very little. The humidity will supply the moisture needed. Watch for rotting of the base, which will indicate too much water.

RIGHT:
Vriesia splendens is a beautiful and spectacular bromeliad, often known as Flaming Sword. It bears large strap-like leaves, banded brown and soft green. From the base of the plant emerges a flower spike, topped with a bright scarlet, spear-shaped bract.

Bulbs and corms

Most bulbs that are planted for home decoration are winter and spring flowering, and they are especially useful because they bloom at a time when little else is in flower. Hyacinths, daffodils and crocuses are frequently grown indoors, but there are many other interesting and charming plants that are also worth trying, such as the dainty blue and white chionodoxa (Glory of the Snow) and the golden-yellow eranthis, both small plants that will make a cheerful show if grown outdoors in pans and brought inside to flower.

Although all the bulbs in this chapter will flower well indoors, many of the hardy spring-flowering types must be kept cool in the early stages of growth. Small bulbs such as snowdrops and grape hyacinths do not take kindly to forcing, and they are best grown in pots in a cold frame and brought indoors when they come into flower.

Some of the larger bulbs such as hyacinths, tulips and daffodils will respond well to forcing — especially if they have been treated for forcing when you buy them.

Bulbs will be equally happy in bulb fibre or soil, but fibre must be used if the containers have no drainage. Ideally, the pots should be wrapped in newspaper or put in a polythene bag, then placed outside and covered with about 15 cm (6 in) of sand, peat or even fine soil. If that isn't possible, keep them in the coolest part of the house. Those indoors should be watched to be sure the soil or fibre does not dry out. Once some top growth is developing, the containers need to be brought indoors and kept at about 10°C (50°F). Don't be tempted to keep them any warmer until buds are showing, when they should be kept in a temperature of about 15–21°C (60–70°F).

Although it is natural to think of bulbs as spring-flowering there are many other interesting subjects to grow in the home at other times of the year. It is quite feasible to grow suitable lilies, such as *Lilium regale* and *L. auratum*, indoors for summer flowering; and the Scarborough Lily (*Vallota speciosa*) is a superb autumn-flowering bulb. There are other good bulbs to choose from that will give pleasure at different times of the year.

Although all the plants in this chapter are popularly called bulbs, some are in fact corms or tubers. A bulb is a thickened, generally underground, bud having a flat basal stem and neatly packed layers of fleshy leaves which have converted to non-green storage organs. If an onion is cut in half this can be seen quite clearly.

Corms, such as gladioli and crocuses, are really swollen stems, and if one is cut across a solid mass of tissue will be seen, without the clearly defined layers of the onion. Tubers are usually underground stems or roots with eyes or buds near their surface (an aconite is one example), and are often of a more irregular shape than bulbs or corms.

Some bulbs, such as daffodils, require staking to prevent the foliage spilling ungainly on neighbouring plants. This can often be done by placing four or five split-cane stakes in the soil around the sides of the pot, and twining strong cotton around them.

Liliums require individual staking, each flowering stem being treated and supported separately. Thin split-canes can be used, and hidden among the foliage.

Tulips often need similar treatment to daffodils. However, only stake them if the stems are too weak to support the blooms. With all staking, it should be unobtrusive, blending with flowers and foliage.

Most bulbs flower well indoors when freshly purchased, but do not expect them to go on flowering the next year without feeding. Hardy bulbs should be planted out in the garden to recuperate.

Allium*

Ornamental Onion. Asia/Southern Europe.
Although not all are true bulbs, several varieties
are suitable for alpine or cold greenhouses, or
can be brought indoors for a short period when
in flower. The flowers are in umbels and the
foliage is strap-shaped; the characteristic family
smell is only apparent when the bulbs are lifted
or the leaves bruised. The whole family appreciate good drainage and full sun. Recommended
kinds are *A. beesianum*, bright blue, 23–30 cm
(9–12 in); *A. cyaneum*, brilliant turquoise blue,
23–30 cm (9–12 in); *A. flavum*, bright yellow,
30–39 cm (12–15 in); *A. moly*, golden-yellow,
broad flat leaves, 15–30 cm (6–12 in); and *A.
narcissiflorum*, pinkish-purple, flowers pendulous, 20–30 cm (8–12 in). All these are summer flowering but *A. neapolitanum*, white, 20–
30 cm (8–12 in) tall, flowers in spring.

Anemone*

Windflower. Greece.
Anemone blanda can be grown under cold conditions in a frame or alpine house, when it will
flower through late winter to mid-spring, with
starry blue, mauve, pink or white flowers on
10–15 cm (4–6 in) stems. The deeply cut leaves
resemble those of a buttercup. The tubers should
be planted 5 cm (2 in) deep in rich soil and
grown in full sun, or a light window. Propagation by division.

Babiana**

South Africa.
Funnel-shaped flowers, sometimes fragrant,
and tapering flat leaves make Babiana an
attractive houseplant. Insert four or five 2·5 cm
(1 in) deep in a 10 cm (4 in) pot of sandy soil
with a little well-rotted manure at the base.
They bloom late winter to spring and then
should be dried off gradually so as to ripen the
corms. *B. stricta* is the best species with 15–30
cm (6–12 in) stems carrying several flowers
with six segments – three of which are white
and three blue with darker blue blotches.
Varieties have cream, crimson and brilliant
blue flowers. Give a light situation indoors.
Propagation by seed or offsets.

Brodiaea**

North and South America.
Brodiaea are sun-loving Californians with grassy
leaves which die away before the umbels of
tubular flowers appear in summer.

They thrive in a good light and rich loam
soil, being particularly suitable for bright office
windows or cool greenhouses. *B. californica* is
lilac-pink, 60 cm (2 ft); *B. ida-maia*, the floral
firecracker, has umbels of long crimson flowers
tipped with yellow and green on 45 cm (18 in)
stems and *B. laxa*, the grass nut, has umbels of
violet-blue or white flowers up to 30 cm (1 ft)
across on 60 cm (2 ft) stems.

ABOVE:
Allium oreophilum *is more
often planted out in the rock
garden or border edge, but it
is a charming plant that can
also brighten the home in
May with its globular heads
of pink flowers. Do not force
the bulb in too much heat.*

93

Calochortus**

Mariposa Lily or Butterfly Tulip. North America. These beautiful bulbous plants have three 'petalled' tulip-shaped flowers, several to a stem in mid-summer. The segments are usually prominently blotched with other colours near the flower bases. Calochortus are very suitable for pan culture in a cool greenhouse or short sojourns indoors. They must have sharp drainage, plenty of water in the growing season and a good baking when the flowers are done. *C. venustus* has white, yellow, purple or red flowers with contrasting blotches, 60 cm (2 ft); and *C. uniflorus* has lilac-pink flowers veined with crimson, 30–45 cm (12–18 in).

Propagate by seed or division.

Chionodoxa*

Glory of the Snow. Europe/Asia.
Chionodoxa is a delightful early blooming bulb for window-boxes, alpine pans or mixing with eranthis, tulips or narcissi in fancy bowls.

It is so charming that it is worth potting a few in a pan in autumn, and bringing them on a little early, to flower just as you're beginning to think that winter is never going to end.

The brilliant blue starry flowers are in a loose cluster, 15 cm (6 in) or more tall, with narrow leaves surrounding them. Large bulbs produce several flowering stems.

Plant the bulbs 3·75 cm (1½ in) deep in any good well drained soil. *C. luciliae* is the most common species and has a pink form 'Pink Giant'. *C. sardensis* is brilliant blue with almost navy blue buds, 15–20 cm (6–8 in). Propagate by seed or division.

Clivia*

Kaffir Lily. Natal.
Clivia miniata makes a splendid houseplant and can exist for years in the same pot if fed during the growing season. Broad, glossy, evergreen strap-shaped leaves are attractive at all times and in spring the plant produces its stout 60 cm (2 ft) stems carrying umbels of large, funnel-shaped flowers with yellow throats. In the type they are light salmon-red but deeper red and yellow forms exist. Under good conditions these are succeeded by scarlet berries.

Clivias do not form proper bulbs, but build up layers of fleshy leaf bases which become rounded and bulb-like in time. New leaves develop in pairs, so that, in the end, a kind of central system is formed from the leaves. A 10-year-old plant can have as many as eight or nine flower-heads, each with a dozen flowers.

Temperature and watering are the two cultivation points to take particular care with. In winter the temperature should not rise above 14°C (58°F), and is better if kept nearer 10°C (about 50°F). It can drop to 7°C (45°F), if the plant is kept slightly dry. In summer moderate warmth is preferred, in the 15–20°C (60–70°F) range.

Colchicum*
Naked Boys. Europe/Asia Minor.

Colchicums are mostly autumn-flowering, tuberous rooted plants with showy, goblet-shaped flowers like giant crocuses. They appear without the leaves – which follow on 30 cm (1 ft) stems with the seedpods in spring – hence the common name.

They should be planted 5 cm (2 in) deep in late summer, in good potting soil and deep pots. They can also be successfully flowered dry, without soil or water, but naturally deteriorate unless planted soon afterwards. *C. autumnale* has starry petalled, rosy-lilac or white flowers; *C. speciosus*, rosy-purple, has larger and more globular flowers. Good cultivars from the last include 'Album', white; 'Disraeli', deep mauve with darker markings; 'Waterlily', fully double, rosy-mauve and 'The Giant', mauve-pink with a white base. The normal height is around 8–15 cm (3–6 in). *C. luteum*, with 2·5 cm (1 in) yellow flowers, blooms in late winter.

Propagation is by seed or division.

Colchicum is a bulb that has been valued not only for its decorative value, but also for its medicinal and culinary virtues. In the past it has been known to be used to elleviate or cure gout, while in the Near East it was often used as a soothing remedy for pains in the joints. It was said to be a sedative which acted upon all of the secreting organs, and was apt to cause depression in large doses, when it acted as an irritant poison.

Convallaria majalis*
Lily-of-the-Valley. Europe/Asia/North America.

Lilies-of-the-Valley can be induced to flower out of season by forcing retarded crowns. These are usually sold in bundles of 25 and on arrival should be loosely planted together in peat, light soil or vermiculite. Keep them in a warm, 24°C (75°F), dark place – such as a covered propagating frame or an airing cupboard – for about four days. They should then be brought into the light and a temperature of 10–13°C (50–55°F) to flower. Some people plant them separately at this time. They will flower in three weeks.

Crocus*

Asia Minor/Adriatic coast/Alps.

A bowl of yellow crocus flowering in mid winter for several weeks is, like the chionodoxas, good for the morale. Yellow is a lovely cheerful colour, and is supposed to be the sign of hope. There are crocuses in other colours as well as shades of purple, violet and almost blue, some most delicately veined and feathered with purple on white, some with petals bronze on the outside and white inside, others whose stamens are bright orange inside a deep purple cup. Some crocuses have pointed petals, some are rounded, so that they look like an elongated egg before they unfold.

The best ones for gentle forcing are the Dutch kinds, which flower in early spring, but the prettiest are those flowering naturally in mid to late winter, which come in the *Crocus chrysanthus* group. Don't forget the autumn-flowering species such as the purple-blue *C. speciosus*, and *C. sativus*, the source of saffron, with its purple flowers.

Crocuses need a gritty compost and are planted 5 cm (2 in) deep and 2·5 cm (1 in) apart in early autumn, except for the autumn-flowering kinds, which are planted in mid summer. Those for forcing are put outdoors in a cool place, plunged in soil and covered with bracken, ashes or leaves. Take precautions against mice.

Eranthis*

Winter Aconite. Europe.

Eranthis is a very easy, tuberous-rooted member of the buttercup family, with bright golden, chalice-shaped flowers set off by 'toby dog' ruffs of pale green, deeply cut, leafy bracts. They bloom in early winter and make delightful subjects for pans in an alpine house or tubs and window boxes.

Damp soil is essential and the tubers should be set 5 cm (2 in) deep. *E. hyemalis* is the easiest and when left undisturbed spreads by means of self-set seedlings. It grows 5–10 cm (2–4 in)

tall. *E.* × *tubergenii* has larger and deeper gold flowers on 8–13 cm (3–5 in) stems but is sterile.

Erythronium**

Trout Lily. North America/Asia/Europe.

Erythroniums can be planted 10 cm (4 in) deep in pans of potting soil with extra peat added and must be kept cool and damp and in partial shade during the summer months. The roots must never dry out. *E. americanum* has pale to deep gold flowers with reflexed petals like a cyclamen, basally marked and flushed outside with red.

The tongue-like leaves are beautifully blotched with chocolate. *E. dens-canis* is the Dog's Tooth Violet (so called because of the shape of the tubers). It has purple blotched leaves and pink, crimson or purple flowers with reflexed petals and deeper basal markings. *E. tuolumnense* has plain green leaves and two or three large, deep yellow flowers on 15 cm (6 in) stems. 'Pagoda' is a more vigorous form with larger flowers on 30 cm (1 ft) stems and a fine cultivar of disputed origin is 'White Beauty' which is white with dark red basal markings.

Erythroniums flower in spring and are not really suitable for house cultivation; they are better in a cold greenhouse or alpine house.

Galanthus nivalis*

Snowdrop. Europe.

Single and double snowdrops can be grown indoors or in pans in alpine houses but must not be subjected to much heat or the bulbs go blind. Grow them in good loam soil mix and keep them from strong sunlight through glass or direct heat. A north window and temperature around 10–13°C (50–55°F) is ideal.

Propagation is by seed or bulb division.

Hippeastrum*

South America.

Hippeastrums are frequently but erroneously known as amaryllis, and are outstanding winter-flowering bulbs with funnel-shaped flowers of great substance and in striking colours – pink, rose, red, scarlet and white, frequently with narrow white petal streaks or mottlings of other shades. Up to four blooms are borne at the tops of 60 cm (2 ft) stems, each flower up to 13 cm (5 in) long and 10 cm (4 in) across when open. The flat strap-shaped leaves are more or less evergreen, although for convenience mature bulbs are usually dried off and rested in summer. Seedlings, however, should be kept going until the bulbs reach flowering size.

Prepared bulbs will flower around Christmas time. Start them by soaking the lower parts of the bulbs in tepid water for four to five days, then pot them singly in good loam, leafmould (equal parts) with enough silver sand to make the compost friable. Half the bulb should be left exposed. Bottom heat encourages vigorous growth so stand them on a warm mantelpiece, a shelf over a radiator or in a cupboard until they get going. They should then be placed in a good light to develop and flower. Little water should be given for the first two weeks and after that only a little on top of the soil.

After flowering, remove the dead flowerhead, and feed with a potash-high feed until the leaves begin to die down; continue to water and keep the plant in a sunny place. If the leaves do not die off, gradually give less water and feed from late summer until the plant is completely dried off, so forcing it to rest from about mid autumn to the beginning of February.

Alternatively, some gardeners keep the plant growing in autumn, but without food after the summer, and repot in fresh compost in winter. Increase is by offsets, though they are slow to reach flowering size.

Hyacinthus orientalis*
Hyacinth. West Asia/Eastern Europe.
Hyacinths are easy to grow, the foliage is attractive, the flowers showy and in vivid colours and they are delightfully fragrant. Roman hyacinths are not a distinct species but a form of *H. orientalis* with slender stems and looser flower spikes. They come in pink, blue and white and usually bloom earlier than the sturdier Dutch hyacinths, which also have a wider colour range. Multiflora hyacinths are other derivatives, characterized by several graceful spikes from every bulb and there are also cynthella or miniature hyacinths only 13–15 cm (5–6 in) tall — ideal for window-boxes.

Hyacinths can be grown in ordinary potting soil, loamless mix, bulb fibre (best for fancy bowls with no drainage holes), newspaper and bulb glasses. Fertilizers are unnecessary but apply water regularly to keep the soil moist.

Representative of specially prepared forcing bulbs for Christmas and New Year flowering are: 'Carnegie' and 'L'Innocence', white; 'Yellow Hammer', yellow; 'Lady Derby' and 'Rosalie', pink; 'Jan Bos' and 'Amsterdam', red; 'Blue Giant', 'Delft Blue' and 'Ostara', blue.

Ipheion uniflorum*
Spring Flower. South America.
Ipheion uniflorum is known as *Brodiaea uniflora* and *Triteleia uniflora*. This is a pretty plant from Peru and Argentina with tufts of lax grassy leaves and many smooth 10–15 cm (4–6 in) stems terminating in single, fragrant, pale violet flowers in spring. Suitable for growing indoors in pots and bowls like crocuses or in alpine houses and cold extensions.

Iris*
Northern Hemisphere.
Several dwarf irises are suitable for window-boxes or growing in pots in the home or alpine house, but they will not tolerate hard forcing so keep them cool (in a garden plunge, cellar or shed) for about eight weeks and then bring them into temperatures of around 10–13°C (50–55°F) to flower.

Iris danfordiae has fragrant lemon-yellow flowers on 8 cm (3 in) stems in winter (February). *I. reticulata*, in character a few weeks later, has violet-scented, dark purple-blue flowers with prominent gold markings on the falls on 10 cm (5 in) stems.

Named varieties of this include 'Cantab', cornflower-blue; 'J. S. Dijt', reddish-purple; and 'Harmony', rich blue.

These irises are so easily grown there is really no excuse for not trying them. The main point to remember is the time of planting, in late summer, which can be rather difficult as the winter seems so far away then as to be unlikely to come. Being tiny, they are best put into pans or small troughs so that they are not overwhelmed. Plant the bulbs about 3·5 cm (1½ in) deep in a standard compost with some coarse sand added, as they like good drainage.

Place them outdoors in a cool shady place until mid autumn and then bring them in, but keep them cool, about 7°C (45°F). When the leaves begin to show, give the plants as much

RIGHT:
Ipheion uniflorum, the Spring Flower, is a pretty plant originating from Peru and Argentina, with tufts of grassy leaves and pale violet flowers in spring. It is ideal for pots and bowls.

RIGHT, BELOW:
Winter-flowering bulbs are a delight to behold during the dull months of winter. One of these brighteners is Iris reticulata, with scented and almost purple-blue flowers. They are ideal for small pots and pans in a cool conservatory or alpine house.

light as possible, otherwise the leaves will tower over the flowers, and give a little warmth as the flower stems elongate.

Lilium**
Lily. Japan/China.

Mid-century hybrid lilies which bloom in late winter make welcome houseplants. The treated bulbs arrive in early winter (December) and should be immediately planted in leafmould, loam and coarse sand (equal parts) with a little crushed charcoal.

Allow three bulbs to a 15 cm (6 in) pot and cover them with 5—8 cm (2—3 in) of soil. Keep them in full light and a temperature around 20°C (70°F).

Varieties include 'Brandywine', apricot-yellow; 'Cinnabar', maroon-red; 'Enchantment', cherry-red; 'Paprika', deep crimson; and 'Prosperity', lemon-yellow.

Many other lilies make good pot plants for summer flowering especially *L. regale* and hybrids, *L. longiflorum* and *L. auratum*. All demand a rich soil mix consisting of equal parts loam, peat, leafmould and well decayed cow-manure with enough coarse sand to ensure good drainage. Use 15 cm (6 in) pots, cover the bulbs with 3·5 cm (1½ in) of soil mix and grow them along in a cool place, shaded from direct sun until the buds appear. They can then go into a warm room to flower.

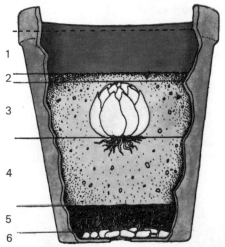

LEFT:
The illustration shows the correct depth when planting a lily bulb: 1. This leaves adequate space for subsequently top-dressing the bulb. 2. A layer of good compost is required above the bulb. 3. The bulb surrounded by compost. 4. A layer of compost beneath the bulb. 5. Rough compost or lumpy peat. 6. Stones or broken pieces of clay pots over the drainage hole.

LEFT:
Mid-century hybrid lilies blooming in late winter bring life and cheerfulness to the winter's end. Here, the variety 'Imperial Crimson' is a delight to see. When in flower, keep them in a warm place, and ensure they are adequately watered, but not standing in it.

Muscari*

Grape Hyacinth. Europe/Asia.

These popular bulbs are sometimes known as Starch Lilies because the mucilaginous bulb sap was once used for starching linen. Easiest to grow indoors are *M. botryoides* 'Album', which has compact cones of small grape-like, white, fragrant flowers on 15–25 cm (6–10 in) stems and the brilliant blue *M. armeniacum*, also fragrant, and its attractive double blue cultivar 'Blue Spire'.

Plant these 2·5 cm (1 in) deep in pots of good soil mix and keep in a cool place – 4°C (39°F) for six to eight weeks before bringing them into higher temperatures 10–13°C (50–55°F) to flower.

Narcissus*

Daffodil. Southern Europe.

The daffodils and narcissi are winter- or early-spring-flowering bulbs, mostly hardy, which take very well to being grown indoors in containers such as pots or troughs. The miniatures such as *Narcissus bulbocodium*, the hoop petticoat daffodil, and *N. cyclamineus*, whose petals reflex backwards just like those of the cyclamen,

can be grown in pans, and are only 10–13 cm (4–5 in) tall.

Plant the bulbs of the normal-sized narcissi so that the 'noses' just show, if in pots, but buried if in troughs (this also applies to the miniatures). Allow a depth of container of at least 13 cm (5 in) if you wish them to flower again the following year, though the prepared kinds will not do so without a season to build up. Pans 10 cm (4 in) deep will be quite suitable for the miniatures.

Use standard potting compost and put the bulbs five to a 13 cm (5 in) diameter pot, or at about 3·5 cm (1½ in) apart in a trough or other container. Don't make the compost too firm, especially just beneath the bulbs.

Prepared bulbs for Christmas flowering have to be planted in early autumn (October) and need eight or nine weeks in a plunge bed outdoors or a cool, dark but frost-free place inside – 4°C (39°F). Unprepared or ordinary bulbs should go in earlier (September) for New Year flowers, or October for February blooms, and need 10 or 12 weeks in cold darkness. There is no other difference in cultivation except this one of timing. At the end of these periods take

them into a good light and temperature of 10–13°C (50–55°F) for flowering. The bulbs can then be given plenty of water.

Suitable kinds for Christmas flowering include 'Golden Harvest' and 'Unsurpassable', both yellow trumpets; 'Yellow Sun', a large-cupped; 'Barrett Browning', small-cupped; 'Texas', a double; 'Peeping Tom', a cylamineus hybrid, and 'Cragford', 'Soleil d'Or' and 'Paper White', Tazetta hybrids.

Scilla*
Squill. Southern Europe/USSR/Iran.
Several miniature scillas are suitable for window-boxes and pot cultivation. S. bifolia has five to seven star-shaped flowers of turquoise blue (or occasionally white or pink) on 20 cm (8 in) stems; S. sibirica has brilliant prussian-blue bells about 2·5 cm (1 in) across on 8–10 cm (3–4 in) stems, and the 10 cm (4 in) S. mischtschen-koana (S. tubergeniana) is very pale blue with an attractive deep blue stripe down the centre of each petal.

All scillas associate pleasingly with snow-drops or miniature narcissi and can be grown in bulb fibre or bowls of light soil mix. Keep them

cool – 4°C (39°F) – for six to eight weeks before bringing them into warm rooms to flower.

Sparaxis**
Harlequin Flower. South Africa.
These variable members of the iris family are best grown in pots or in raised beds in a cool greenhouse. The flowers resemble freesias somewhat in white, yellow, orange, red or purple shades, always with yellow throats. They bloom in early summer and have grassy leaves.

Plant the corms 8–10 cm (3–4 in) deep and the same distance apart in light soil mix. After the foliage dies down, dry the corms and store them in a dry place until planting time comes round again in late autumn (November).

Tulipa**
Tulip. Europe.
Tulips make good pot plants for indoor cultivation but only when the roots have had a long session (14–16 weeks) in cold darkness. Too often this procedure is scamped with inevitable and disappointing results. Ordinary unprepared bulbs should be planted in late summer (early September to mid-October) in good potting mix and kept in temperatures around 9°C (49°F) for 10 to 12 weeks. A plunge bed out of doors is best but failing that a dark frost-free cellar, shed or room. They should then be brought into warm darkness – 15°C (60°F) – for two or three weeks and only after this taken into a light living room to flower.

Specially prepared bulbs for Christmas flowering are planted before the middle of September, kept cool as before until the first week in December, then taken into temperatures of 18°C (64°F) for a few days until growth is apparent. All this time they should be in darkness but may then go into light to flower.

Good forcing kinds are: early singles, 'Bellona', golden yellow, 45 cm (18 in); 'Brilliant Star', scarlet, 30 cm (1 ft); 'Doctor Plesman', orange-red, 36 cm (14 in); early doubles, 'Wilhelm Kordes', orange-yellow flushed red, 30 cm (1 ft); 'Orange Nassau', blood-red, 30 cm (1 ft); 'Electra', cherry-red, 30 cm (1 ft); 'Murillo Max', white flushed pink, 36 cm (14 in); and 'Mr Van der Hoef', golden-yellow, 30 cm (1 ft).

Vallota**
Scarborough Lily. South Africa.
Vallota speciosa, a superb autumn-flowering amaryllid, does well in pots and bowls and looks most arresting in a fireplace with concealed lighting, on a pedestal stand or on a conservatory bench.

Growing about 60 cm (2 ft tall), the 8 cm (3 in) funnel-shaped blooms are vivid scarlet with prominent golden stamens. They are carried in umbels of four to ten on each stem. The leaves are long and narrow. Vallotas should be planted in loam, sand and leafmould (equal parts) and are helped by an occasional feed during the growing season. They can be lifted, divided and repotted every three or four years.

Increasing plants

There are several ways of raising house plants, or of increasing your present range of plants. The most common way is by cuttings, especially with foliage plants. Propagation by leaf cuttings is an easy way of increasing some plants, such as begonias and African Violets.

Plants like sansevierias, aspidistras and clivias may be increased by division of the root when it has made a sufficient number of growths.

Many house plants grown for their flowers, and also a number of foliage plants, are raised from seed.

A fourth way of increasing your stock is to detach and plant the small plantlets which are produced on the parent plants. The Pick-a-back Plant, *Tolmiea menziesii*, and *Chlorophytum comosum* are propagated in this way.

Air layering is sometimes practised for rooting a shoot of a large shrubby plant like ficus.

Cuttings
Cuttings may be taken from either the stem or the leaf of the plant. Many cuttings will not root unless placed in a warm and humid atmosphere. This may be artificially provided by using a propagating case.

It is possible to buy plastic seed trays which have dome-like covers. Some of the plastic covers have adjustable ventilators set in the top of the cover. Propagating cases can also be bought with electric heating capable of maintaining temperatures of 20–27°C (70–80°F) which are desirable for raising seeds of certain types of tropical plants. For most cuttings, however, ordinary room temperatures of around 20°C (70°F) are satisfactory.

An improvised propagator can be made by filling either a box or a large flower pot with the cutting medium and then bending pieces of wire into a half circle and pushing the ends into the pot. After the cuttings have been inserted in the potting mix, drape thin clear plastic over the wires and tie it round the pot.

Most stem cuttings consist of young unflowered shoots about 8–10 cm (3–4 in) long. The lowest pair of leaves is removed and a clean

Propagation

Houseplants are quite easily and inexpensively increased by seed, cuttings, or even just pegging part of the plant into a rooting compost.

Seed can be sown in a pot or other container which has a layer of crocks in its base, covered with a well-drained seed compost. Sow the seed thinly, cover lightly and gently water them in. Cover individual pots with a plastic bag, or collectively by placing them in a large box and covering the top with a pane of glass. Keep the seeds warm and moist and in a dark place until they germinate, then give them full light. When large enough to be handled, the seedlings can be pricked-out into small pots holding a potting compost.

Plants such as chlorophytum and Saxifraga sarmentosa can easily be increased by pegging the small plantlets at the ends of stems into a sandy compost. As soon as the plantlets have rooted, sever them from the parent plant.

104

Increasing plants by leaf cuttings is the normal method for saintpaulias, gloxinias and begonias. Take a young but mature leaf, with its stem, from a parent plant and insert it into a pot containing a mixture of peat and sand. Firm the cutting, place a plastic bag over the pot and place it in a warm place.

Large-leaved begonias may be increased by vein cuttings. To do this, remove a mature leaf, turn it upside down and make several nicks across the veins. Again turn the leaf over and lay it flat on the compost, pegging it firmly in place. Cover the pot with a plastic bag and keep it warm. New plantlets will appear at the cuts in the veins.

Softwood cuttings can be used to increase such plants as pelargoniums and chrysanthemums. Select sideshoots about 10 cm (4 in) long and make a cut cleanly across the stem, just below a leaf. Remove the lower leaves and insert the cutting to about a third of its length in a well-drained rooting compost. Put a plastic bag over the pot and position it in a warm place until the cuttings have rooted.

cut is made with a sharp knife or a razor blade just below the node or joint where the lower leaves were removed. This is the type of cutting made from plants of *pelargonium* (geranium), *hydrangea*, *fuchsia*, *tradescantia*, *cissus* and similar plants.

The prepared shoots are inserted in a mixture of peat and really coarse sand or, as some call it, grit. The fine sticky and yellow sand is not good for this purpose as the object of mixing the sand with the peat is to help drainage and to keep the mixture sweet. For most cuttings, equal parts by bulk of moist peat and sand is a suitable mixture. Or you can buy proprietary peat-based cuttings mixtures. There are also peat-based mixtures which are suitable for seed sowing, rooting cuttings and for potting.

Hormone rooting compounds can be used to hasten rooting. The base of the cutting is dipped in the powder before it is inserted in the rooting medium. Some rooting compounds contain a fungicide which helps to prevent the cutting from rotting at the base. Bruising of the base of the cutting, as often happens if they are cut with secateurs, may encourage rotting. For this reason always use a sharp knife or a razor blade when making and trimming the cuttings.

Make sure the cutting mixture is nicely moist. Insert the cuttings around the inner edge of the flower pot, making a hole with a pencil deep enough to take the bottom 5 cm (2 in) or so of the cutting. Do not make the hole too deep — the base of the cutting should rest on the soil at the bottom of the hole.

When the cuttings have been inserted, and the plastic cover put in place, stand the pot in a light place, but out of direct sunshine.

A pot is really the best receptacle for rooting a small number of cuttings. If a large number is required use a seed box, but do not cram the cuttings in too close together — they should not touch each other. As soon as the cuttings have rooted, put them singly in small pots — 8 cm (3 in) diameter is a good size for the first potting.

Short shoots, about 10 cm (4 in) long, of some foliage plants such as ivy and *impatiens* (Busy Lizzie), will produce roots if the stems are inserted for about 5 cm (2 in) of their length in water. When they have produced roots 2·5 cm (1 in) or so in length they may be inserted carefully in a small pot — 8 cm (3 in) diameter — of potting soil.

The propagative technique called air layering can be used to increase such plants as camellias, hibiscus and Ficus elastica. It is a technique well suited to plants that have grown too tall and lost their lower leaves. First, make a slit in the bark, just below a leaf joint, and dust the area with rooting powder. Tie a piece of plastic around the stem, about 7 cm (3 in) below the slit, and pack moist peat around the stem. Securely tie the top of the plastic. As soon as small roots show through the moist peat, sever the stem just below the roots and pot the rooted cutting into a larger pot.

Leaf Cuttings

A number of plants, notably *saintpaulia*, *streptocarpus* and *begonia* may be propagated by leaf cuttings. With *saintpaulia*, the African Violet, a leaf with a length of stem is used, and the bottom 2·5 cm (1 in) or so of stem is inserted in the cutting medium. African Violet leaves will also make roots if the bottom 2·5 cm (1 in) or so of stem is inserted in water. *Streptocarpus* leaves are cut right across horizontally in sections about 2·5–5 cm (1–2 in) wide. These are inserted in the soil vertically.

Leaves of large-leaved begonias and similar foliage forms may be treated in different ways. A whole leaf may be laid on the surface of the cutting medium, and cuts made through the veins at a distance of about 5 cm (2 in) apart with a razor blade or a sharp knife. Small stones are placed at intervals on the leaf, or pegs of bent wire are used, to keep the cut surfaces in contact with the soil.

Alternatively, small pieces of leaf about the size of a large postage stamp, each piece containing a section of a vein, may be laid on the rooting medium or inserted in it to half their depth vertically. The cuttings, leaves or leaf sections must be kept moist and in a temperature of 18–24°C (64–75°F). They will root best if kept in a propagating case or in a box covered with a sheet of glass or plastic film.

Air Layering

This is a favourite method of propagating certain types of plant with a woody stem, such as the rubber plant, *Ficus elastica*, or cordylines.

At a point, say 60 cm (2 ft) below the top of the shoot, make an upward slit in the stem about 2·5–4 cm (1–1½ in) long. Wedge the slit open with a sliver of wood. Additionally, if desired, remove a narrow circle of bark about 12 mm (½ in) wide round the stem just above the slit. Dust this area liberally with rooting compound. Then wrap thin plastic film round the stem, tying it below the slit. The film should be wide enough and overlapping so that it forms a kind of cylindrical 'bag' over the cut part. Fill this pouch with moist sphagnum moss or moist peat, and then tie it to the stem above the cut. In about 10 weeks roots should grow from the wounded area, and the stem may then be severed from the parent plant and the new plant potted carefully.

BELOW:
Impatiens petersiana *or* Busy Lizzie *is an excellent plant to grow from seed, or from cuttings. This is a plant that roots very easily, even in water.*

Plantlets

Several plants we may grow in the home produce tiny plantlets on their leaves, or on stems or stolons. These little plantlets may be detached carefully and rooted in a pot or box of cutting medium. Some plantlets, such as those that appear on stems produced on plants of *Chlorophytum comosum*, may be left until they are say 5 cm (2 in) high before they are detached. Those produced at the top of the leaf stalk on *Tolmiea menziesii* are detached as soon as they are large enough to handle.

Another plant that produces small plantlets is *Saxifraga sarmentosa* (*S. stolonifera*) commonly known as Mother of Thousands, Aaron's Beard, Roving Sailor or Strawberry Geranium. The red creeping stems or stolons are produced from the heart of the plant, and these bear the young plantlets which root easily.

A succulent plant easy to grow in the home is *Bryophyllum daigremontianum*. It produces many tiny plantlets around the edges of the leaves. These may be detached when they are quite small – 6–12 mm ($\frac{1}{4}-\frac{1}{2}$ in) across, and 'sown' or scattered on the cutting or seed sowing mix in a pot, and kept warm and moist. They root very easily.

Division

A few plants are propagated by division of the crowns, or by separating 'offset' shoots as in sansevierias. Prise the soil away from the ball of soil and loosen the roots as much as possible. Then with a sharp knife separate and sever where necessary young well rooted pieces of the old plant. Pot these separately.

Seed

Many flowering plants such as *cyclamen*, *clivia*, *impatiens* and *begonia* are easily raised from seed provided one has the space on a windowsill or on a bench near a window. Many foliage plants too may be raised from seeds – *coleus*, *ficus*, *pilea* and *grevillea* among them.

It is also possible to raise young plants from date and peach stones, orange and lemon pips, and the seed of the avocado pear. This gives a certain amount of interest and pleasure, but eventually the plants become too large for a living-room and have to be discarded.

As with propagation by cuttings, no elaborate equipment is necessary, although it helps to have a heated propagating case that can be kept at a temperature of 20–27°C (70–80°F). Failing this, a pot or box with a plastic cover may be stood near a radiator or in another warm situation to maintain a steady degree of heat. It is not necessary to exclude light from the seed pot or box. The reason gardeners cover their seed pots or boxes with brown paper is to keep them shaded from strong sun and from drying out unnecessarily. Naturally, as soon as the seeds are seen to have germinated, they must be brought into the light.

Fill the pot or box with a seed sowing mixture, either one based on loam, or a peat-based mix. Level it very gently by pressing a flat board on the surface, but on no account consolidate the mixture – just make an even level surface. Sow the seeds very thinly. With fine seeds it helps to mix them with fine dry sand before sowing. Just cover the seed with fine sifted soil or fine sand.

When the seedlings have opened two leaves, prick them off – that is, transplant them into another box, or singly into very small 2·5–5 cm (1–2 in) diameter pots. Later on they will be transferred to 8–9 cm (3–3$\frac{1}{2}$ in) pots in which they should pass their first year or 18 months. After seedlings have been pricked off shade them from strong light, and of course see that they never dry out. The roots of seedlings are very easily damaged if allowed to become dry.

Cactus seeds are often sold as a mixture of as many as a dozen species or varieties. These often germinate over a long period – months even. So, as the seedlings appear, carefully remove them, using the tip of a penknife blade, as they become large enough, and pot them singly in small pots.

The flat seeds of the attractive foliage plant *Grevillea robusta* germinate best if they are inserted in the soil edgewise.

FAR RIGHT:
The Spider Plant, Chlorophytum comosum, *is really spectacular when mature and large. The small plantlets cascade around the mother plant, and these can be used to provide new plants by pegging them into small pots.*

BELOW:
Saxifraga sarmentosa (S. stolonifera) *is commonly called the Mother of Thousands. It is a plant that can be easily increased by pegging the small runners into pots of compost.*

Keeping plants healthy

2

1

Although you might imagine that pests and diseases are the cause of so many plant problems, it is, in fact, the physiological disorders or cultural faults which claim the largest toll of indoor plant failures.

Physiological disorders or cultural faults are by definition problems that affect the plant due to where it is grown, how it is grown and what we may do to the plant. This includes over-watering, under-watering, sun scald, cold water scald, physical damage, draughts, temperature fluctuation, low humidity and misuse of aerosols.

Low Humidity
Plants that originate in warm and humid conditions are particularly susceptible to dry, arid conditions. Leaf tips and edges are the first to suffer, turning brown and dehydrating.

Plants continually lose water from their leaves by the process of transpiration in an effort to stop the leaf tissue from over-heating. If the atmosphere is excessively dry, the plant continues losing water, often at a higher level than it can compensate for by absorbing water through the roots. The result is that the last part of the plant to receive water is the first to lose it and thus dehydration occurs.

The brown tips and edges can be trimmed back, but this does not solve the problem, only masks the effect.

In order to obviate the problem an attempt must be made to raise the humidity around the plant by plunging the pot into a tray of a moist medium such as peat or sphagnum moss. The micro-climate thus produced helps the plant to retain water within its tissue.

Over-watering, Under-watering?
Probably more plants die, or at least suffer, from over-watering than from any other problem, and indeed it can be a little difficult to identify immediately whether the plant has been over- or under-watered.

The obvious symptoms of both are that the plant wilts, followed by leaf dehydration and thereafter rapid leaf drop. In both cases this is due to the fact that the plant is not absorbing water. In the dry plant there is obviously little or no water, but with an excessively wet plant,

although there is a super-abundance of water, there are usually no active roots.

The cause of an under-watered plant is obvious but with an over-watered plant the problem is a little more complex. Most people think that to keep a plant healthy, the addition of water to a pot is quite sufficient, with the occasional drop of liquid fertilizer, but the truth is that air is also required. Therefore, with the majority of plants frequent addition of water to an already moist soil mixture quickly displaces any surplus air and an anaerobic or airless soil is produced, to the rapid detriment of the plant.

The roots then suffocate, die and break down, and the plant above dies from dehydration.

A plant that is over-watered and is showing primary signs of stress may be saved by removing it from its pot and letting it dry out. This should take 24—48 hours, after which it can be replaced in the pot and watered.

Over-watering usually happens during the winter, when transpiration is low. Therefore, be extra vigilant during the late autumn and winter — and even early spring.

Sun Scald

When certain plants are exposed to high light intensities, sun scald may result. The damage may take the appearance of dehydrated areas on the leaf surface, for large irregular patches on the leaves usually mean that the plant has been exposed directly to the sun's rays

Cold Water Scorch

This more usually affects plants such as saintpaulias and gloxinias and occurs when a plant is watered with cold instead of tepid water, the water droplets being allowed to remain on the leaves. An unusual marbling effect results looking somewhat similar to the tracks left by the leaf miner in chrysanthemums and cineraria. It is better, therefore, to water these plants from below.

Physical Damage

It is surprising how much physical damage can be caused to a plant, and resultant effect not become apparent for some time. The actual visible result is extremely variable, but tears and splits in the leaf are most common, caused by rough handling.

Probably the most unusual effect of physical damage occurs when the growing point is damaged. Even if the damage to the terminal bud appears slight, as the leaf grows the damage looks more severe and subsequent leaves invisible in the terminal bud at the time of damage may also show some signs of marking if the effect was more than one leaf deep. Eventually the plant will grow through this.

Draughts

The more delicate plants are susceptible to draughts and the usual effect is sudden and rapid leaf drop. On certain plants, however, the effect may be nothing more than drooping of the leaves. Quite obviously if the plant is reacting either way it is in a bad position and should be moved immediately.

Aerosols

Certain aerosols can damage plants, producing minute flecks on the leaf, sometimes with a silvery appearance. Avoid spraying aerosols such as hair lacquer or polish near the plants.

Temperature Fluctuation

This is more of a problem in winter than at any other time as temperatures are more liable to sudden changes. The most usual effect of temperature fluctuation is rapid leaf drop: as much as one-third of the leaves may drop overnight if the fluctuation is excessive.

During the day the room tends to be warmer while it is occupied, but at night the heating is usually lower and the temperature drops. It is not the low temperature which is the causal factor but the temperature difference – relatively high to low temperature in a short time.

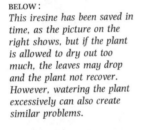

BELOW:
This iresine has been saved in time, as the picture on the right shows, but if the plant is allowed to dry out too much, the leaves may drop and the plant not recover. However, watering the plant excessively can also create similar problems.

Fungal Spots

Under humid conditions certain plants may suffer from fungal spot. Dracaenas, hederas, dieffenbachias and others also may become infected by these. The spot or spots take the appearance of soft brown roughly circular areas. This is not a major problem and is usually an uncommon one and as such prevention is often not thought necessary.

The cure is to spray with benomyl once a week for three weeks. If possible remove infected leaves, although this is not essential if the leaf is only slightly affected.

Grey Mould (*Botrytis cinerea*)

Grey mould starts with brown patches on leaves or stems from which grey fur grows and rotting quickly spreads. It is most likely to break out in cool, damp conditions and following an injury to a plant caused by insect attack, mechanical damage and so on. Cut off the infected part and spray with benomyl.

Mildew

A white powder in patches on the surface of leaves and stems, sometimes also on flowers, is the main symptom of mildew, to which begonias and chrysanthemums are especially prone. It is seen mainly in summer, when plants are dry at the roots, rather enclosed and very warm. Remove affected parts as far as possible, and spray plants with dinocap or benomyl, or dust with flowers of sulphur.

Root Diseases and Damping off

Provided the soil mix is sterile, these diseases should not be a problem unless the soil is kept too moist under cool conditions. The symptoms are wilting of the plant while the soil is still moist, the effects being that of either rotting of the roots or stem.

It is possible to prevent this disease by using a clean soil mixture and good cultural conditions.

The best treatment is to water the soil three times at 10 day intervals, with a solution of benomyl.

Rust and Azalea Gall

Rust takes the form of raised reddish-brown powdery spots underneath leaves. Azalea gall results in thickened and blistered leaves, grey-white in colour, and sometimes also discoloured flowers. Hand removal of diseased leaves and flowers is usually sufficient to keep either disease under control.

Sooty Mould

Sooty mould is a fungus disease which lives and feeds on the honeydew that is produced by the insect pests that suck sap. Sooty mould does not live on plants and does no harm to them. But the mould and the honeydew block the stomata, collect dust and prevent transpiration, so they should be wiped off with a moist cloth.

Greenfly (aphids)

These insect pests are a very successful species. They reproduce extremely rapidly, and are now becoming resistant to various insecticides with which control has previously been achieved. Also called Plant Lice, they are tiny green

FAR LEFT, BELOW:
Botrytis is a fungal disease which attacks the soft parts of plants. Plants susceptible to this are cyclamen, saintpaulias and gloxinias. The fungus appears as a fluffy and greyish mould, which once disturbed produces clouds of spores which spread the infection to other plants.

LEFT:
Damping off is usually well known to most gardeners. The symptoms are wilting of the plant while the soil is still moist. The disease is intensified by keeping the soil far too moist, especially when the air temperature is low.

FAR LEFT, ABOVE:
Fungal Spots may affect plants under certain humid conditions. The spots, or spot, may take on the appearance of soft brown circular areas. This is not usually a major problem and can be prevented quite easily.

113

creatures up to 2 mm ($\frac{1}{8}$ in) long, sometimes with wings. They feed by sucking the sap from a leaf through needle-like mouthparts which are stabbed into the leaf tissue. They move very little, and can be seen clustered at the tips of new shoots, and on the underside of leaves.

Plant growth becomes distorted and stunted. Leaves curl and sometimes turn yellow. New shoots stop growing until the greenfly have gone. Infested plants become weakened. The insects secrete honeydew, a sticky liquid which falls on to leaves, and on which sooty mould can grow.

Thumb-and-finger squashing will get rid of most of them, and sometimes complete removal of a shoot tip is the best solution. Spraying with water under pressure will wash off the rest, or you can spray with an insecticide containing either derris, resmethrin or malathion.

Leaf-miner

The adult leaf-miner is a minute fly, but it is the tiny maggot which does the damage. Eggs are laid on the leaves of plants, and the maggot which hatches eats its way into the leaf tissue, just below the skin, and stays there, moving about as it feeds. Very pale brown or light-green wavy lines and blisters appear on the upper surface of the leaf, and can cover it. Chrysanthemums and cinerarias suffer badly, but almost any plant may be attacked. Remove affected leaves and spray the rest with malathion.

Mealy-bug

The mealy-bug is an almost stationary dark-grey insect which covers itself with a small blob of white fluff and feeds as greenfly do, mainly at stem joints or on bark, or tucked into crevices such as necks of hippeastrum bulbs. Mealy-bugs are often not noticed until there is a big infestation which has done a good deal of damage. Scraping them off with the back of a knife is a good way of dealing with them, and the point can be inserted into awkward parts of the plant where the bugs may be lurking. The young have no protective fluff, but are flattish blobs of

pale brown, red or yellow on the stems, easy to miss. A hand lens or magnifier will help you to see them clearly.

Spray the plant with malathion, or use methylated spirits on individual bugs if the plant is sensitive to malathion.

Red Spider Mite

One of the most frequent and troublesome pests on indoor plants, as the hot dry atmosphere of central heating suits them perfectly, are red spider mites. A hand lens is needed to see them on the underside of the leaf. They are pale yellow or pale red, tiny round pests which suck the sap, and moult their skins as they grow, leaving a white ghost-like replica of themselves behind.

They also produce webbing, which can be seen festooning stems. They take only a month to become adult and lay eggs and increase rapidly during the summer.

Prevent them appearing by always keeping the atmosphere humid and ensuring that the plants never run short of water. Plants which are infested should be thoroughly sprayed with malathion solution, repeating twice more at

about ten-day intervals.

Severely infested plants should be isolated until free of this troublesome pest.

Root Aphis
Root aphis lives in the soil and, like greenfly above ground, it sucks the sap from the plant, but through the roots not the leaves. Root aphis is whitish-grey in colour and will be found on the roots and in the compost.

Treat the plant by washing away from the roots all the compost and root aphis you can see. Then repot in uncontaminated compost. Water with a solution of malathion, and repeat the process about ten days later. For plants sensitive to malathion, use bioresmethrin instead.

Root Mealy-bug
Root mealy-bug attacks the roots of plants, especially the small fine roots. They are easily controlled by drenching the soil in a solution of malathion. For plants sensitive to malathion use bioresmethrin. Treat root mealy-bug on cacti as you would root aphis, using resmethrin for the insecticide.

Scale Insects
Like mealy-bugs, scale insects are immobile, feeding in the same place throughout their lives, protected by a hard horny case, brown, grey or black in colour. The adults lay eggs under the scales and the resultant young move out to their own feeding grounds and grow their own protective shells, which gradually enlarge and darken in colour from pale green.

Their feeding results in the production of large quantities of sticky honeydew, on which sooty mould grows. This and the feeding may weaken a plant considerably. The scales will be found on the stems and bark as well as on the leaves, close to the main veins on the underside. Scrape off gently with the back of a knife on to a sheet of paper beneath, and then spray thoroughly with malathion, repeating twice more at 10-day intervals.

Slugs and Snails
Slugs and snails are most likely to be a problem with windowsill and hanging-basket plants, especially if you see large holes in leaves and lumps missing from stems on any plant, for no apparent reason. They hide during the day and feed at night, so are seldom seen. Look for them in the base of pots, just inside the drainage hole, tucked into the undergrowth of a group of plants, or any kind of crack or crevice near to the damaged plant. Remove and destroy.

Whitefly
Minute, white-winged, fly-like creatures, found on the underside of leaves. The damage is done by the larvae, which are also minute, and look like round, transparent, green scales adhering to the leaf. They suck out their food and produce honeydew in large quantities.

Leaves turn greyish and become very messy and curled in bad attacks, and the plants cease to grow and may die. Remove badly infested parts and spray the remainder several times at intervals of three to four days with bioresmethrin, which destroys the larvae — the adults eventually die naturally.

CENTRE, LEFT:
Root Mealy-bug attacks the roots, grazing on the fine root hairs. They may, in severe cases, cause the foliage of the plant to become yellow and brown. They are, however, soon controlled and killed by watering the soil with a suitable insecticide.

LEFT, ABOVE:
Scale Insects almost look part of the plant, resembling small blisters, usually on the undersides of the leaves. However, in severe infestations they may appear on the upper surfaces.

LEFT, BELOW:
Whitefly are fly-like insects which infest the undersides of leaves. They suck at the plant's juices and excrete honeydew, making the plant look unsightly. These insects create a further eye-sore by shedding their skins, which cling to the plant and resemble ghost insects.

Special effects

Plants can be used for many special purposes in the home, but the basic reason is usually to create interest and colour. The positioning of the plants is therefore very important, whether they are in window-boxes, hanging baskets, trays, bottles, or singly on their own. Suggestions on how to get that 'something extra' from plants is given in this chapter.

Window Displays
One of the difficulties with window displays is the problem of deciding for whom the display is intended – the owner or the man in the street looking in. But however the display is arranged, the looker-in is likely to get the best from it, as almost all the plants will quite quickly turn their leaves to the natural light source.

The occasional twist of the pot will, of course, help to improve the internal appearance of the window arrangement. Turning the pot in this way will also keep the more rounded type of plant, such as *Peperomia caperata*, looking less lop-sided.

Before arranging a window display, take into account the light requirements of the plant you intend to use, as there is nothing to be gained from putting shade-loving marantas in window locations that will expose them to the full, albeit filtered, rays of the sun. Similarly, there would be little point in putting sun-loving crotons in windows that face due north.

If there is nothing more than a simple windowledge for placing plants on, ensure that radiators immediately below the windowsill are not in use to damage plants placed immediately above them. Hot air ascending from room

heaters will be harmful to almost all potted plants, and the hot, dry conditions created will be a perfect breeding place for such pests as red spider. One way of overcoming the problem is to place a shelf on top of the radiator which will deflect hot air from the plants.

Where shelf space around the window is limited, a great deal can be done to increase the potential plant area by putting plants in hanging pots.

Many of the trailing green-foliaged plants grow equally well when climbing a supporting stake or trellis, and the majority are sold as climbing plants. They are sold in this way because it is more practical for the producer of the plant to control them when they are neatly tied to a support of some kind.

Fortunately, the majority of the smaller-leaved plants can be carefully removed from their supports and allowed to trail naturally. Following the removal from the support, the plant leaves will have an unnatural appearance, but will quickly adjust to the new position as they turn their leaves to the light source.

Two trailing plants that are not too bulky, so not so demanding in respect of space, are *Saxifraga stolonifera* (Mother of Thousands) and *Ceropegia woodii* (Hearts Entangled), both of which will trail very effectively. The ceropegia has small heart-shaped leaves that are attached to very slender stems that hang straight downwards from the pot and may be several metres (yards) in length. Trailing *Sedum sieboldii* is another good choice.

For the narrow windowsill, trough-type containers are excellent as they blend naturally and you can get many more plants into them, certainly more than if the container had a circular

LEFT:
Window-boxes burgeoning with gaily-coloured plants can look equally spectacular both from the inside and outside of the home. Do ensure that the box is securely fastened to the windowsill, and that the plants can be given adequate water.

BELOW:
Where ever there is a corner, a shelf, or even a dull window, there is a plant that will fit into it. Here, a series of hanging baskets provide an eye-level attraction, while window-boxes house more erect plants, such as dracaenas and cordylines.

RIGHT:
Bay windows can be brightened with such plants as the floriferous impatiens. Small windows filled with flowers give the impression of the window being larger than it actually is. It will be necessary to turn the plant around each day, as its natural tendency will be to grow towards the light and become imbalanced.

BELOW, RIGHT
Cissus antarctica *looks delightful when set on a windowsill and trailed along the upper part of the window. Some form of support will be required, often a thin piece of string or wire being sufficient. Eventually the support will be hidden by the foliage.*

FAR RIGHT, ABOVE:
Plants grouped in front of unused ornamental fire-screens can be eye-catching. Use plants contrasting in height and differing in the shape of their foliage. Here, at the back, is Sansevieria trifasciata, with Asplenium nidus (left) and a maranta. If possible, stand the individual pots in one large and attractive container.

FAR RIGHT, BELOW:
By carefully illuminating small collections of plants, they can be made focal points of interest. Moving the light slightly can make different plants more dominant. Plants under lights are in more warmth and will require additional water.

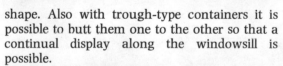

shape. Also with trough-type containers it is possible to butt them one to the other so that a continual display along the windowsill is possible.

Often, the houseplant grower wishing to make the window area a special feature of the room will need a selection of larger plants at either side, to frame the picture as it were.

The size of such plants will, to some extent, be dictated by the area and the height of the window. But whatever the size of the plant, it is important that any framework to which they may be attached (trellis, for example) should be free-standing and not attached to the wall of the room, as plants will then in effect become part of the room. While the plant is growing trouble-free this sort of situation may be all very well, but if pests, for example, become a problem plants should be mobile enough to be moved outside and thoroughly sprayed over.

There is no doubt whatsoever that the best indoor plants are grown in the rooms that have the largest window area in relation to the size of the room, and that the best plants in such rooms will be growing in the vicinity of the window.

Bay windows that are glassed to the floor are probably best of all as there is reasonable scope with such windows for the artistic plant grower to create a really eye-catching array of plants. In such window areas there is an environment that is as near to that of a greenhouse as is ever likely to be in the home. And with a little extra effort the floor area of such windows can be waterproofed so that plants in the window recess can be watered more freely.

Besides the bolder display on the floor there is also the possibility of fixing shelves across the window on which a wide selection of both foliage and flowering plants may be grown. Also, to keep the area surrounding plants cleaner and more agreeable for the plants themselves a metal container fitting exactly into the window recess can be made.

LEFT:
Plants do not necessarily have to be exceptionally large to be dramatic and impressive. Here, the delightful Ficus pumila *is used as a foil, lending interest to the plant stand. Decorative plant holders are useful in such places.*

to a high ceiling that is too far away from the plants to be effective. Where the natural light source is very poor and plants are more dependent on artificial sources, it will be necessary for the lighting to be switched on for at least 12 hours each day. Coloured lights may improve the appearance of some plants, but it is really very much better to avoid strong colours as they can have very odd effects on some plants.

Plant collections arc often seen at their best when darkness descends and lights are switched on above them — unsightly pots and plant stems are lost in the darker, lower area of the plants, and flowers and foliage are highlighted. It is worth the trouble being taken to ensure that indoor plants are provided with artificial lighting that will set them off to best advantage.

Should adaptability be an important advantage as far as lighting is concerned it is advisable to use spotlights that can be adjusted much more readily than fixed light fittings. Spotlights can be used to augment the more permanent lighting, and may be used to highlight particular plants in a collection. But it is important that such lights should be be placed too close to the plants as there is every possibility that foliage will be damaged by the heat that is generated.

Even the humble and solitary plant on the windowsill can have its appearance and performance enhanced by placing it under a wall or table lamp during the evening. But bear in mind when lighting plants for effect for a particular occasion, it is better to err on the side of too little light rather than too much. Harsh lighting that is overdone is much less effective than softer lighting that gives the plants in a collection an air of mystery.

Lighting Plants for Effect

There is nothing less pleasing than the sight of dust-laden plants fighting a losing battle to survive in a corner of a room that is badly lighted and devoid of windows. Plants are attractive features in themselves, and their attraction will be heightened if they are given an important position in which to grow and light to show off their beauty.

By going to some expense and fitting special cabinets with built-in lighting, it is possible for many plants to be grown entirely under artificial light conditions, with no help whatsoever from natural daylight.

By trial and error you will find that a great many plants are suited to this form of culture. The saintpaulia (African Violet) does especially well and may be had in flower throughout the year, with a collection of different varieties.

In larger rooms, where bolder plants are in use, the standard warm white fluorescent tube will be satisfactory, provided it is not attached

Plants to Brighten Dull Spots

It is often supposed that plants are the perfect choice when it comes to selecting something to lighten up that darker corner of the living room, but nothing could be further from the truth. The only foliage plants that are likely to brighten the dark corners are those with highly coloured or variegated foliage, and these are the very plants that will require more than the average amount of light if they are to retain their colouring and prosper.

But this is not to say that there are no plants that are suited to less well-lit conditions, as there are many purely green foliage plants that will fare better in the darker, shaded corner or unused fireplace than they will if placed on the sunny windowsill. Among these you may choose from almost any of the many green-leaved philodendrons, which have either small leaves, in the case of *P. scandens*, or larger leaves, in the case of *P. hastatum*. Most of the bolder types of ferns will also be better placed out of the sun's rays, and the larger types, such as nephrolepis, will fill the space in almost any corner location. The latter, as well as most palms, are at their best when placed on top of one of those superb Victorian-style pedestals, or on top of a wrought-iron pedestal if antique designs are out of the

question. Mention of Victoriana immediately brings to mind the dear old aspidistra which was so much a part of the Victorian interior. *A. elatior* (*lurida*), the Cast Iron Plant, is one of the most durable of potted plants provided a reasonable temperature is maintained. For proper decoration value, however, it depends on a handsome container.

Plants for Corners

If one must have a colourful plant in the darker corner it will be essential to augment the available daylight with an electric lamp of some kind adjacent to the plant. It would be an expensive business to have a plant in each corner of the room with its own electric lamp providing the essential additional amount of light, but for the owner of a number of plants the problem can be solved by grouping the plants together in one corner with one light source catering for all their needs. A group of plants growing together in this way with a light over them will be much more effective and the plants will grow very much better than if they were scattered about the room because plants thrive better in company than singly.

You can purchase or have made wrought iron or bamboo stands that are fitted with a series of rings in which plant pots of varying size can be placed. These rings are set at varying heights on the metal or bamboo stand and can be most effective when a variety of plants are placed in them. A selection of plants placed on a tall stand of this kind will also solve many problems for the householder who has far too many plants in living accommodation that is restricted in respect of space.

When arranging a plant stand of this kind it is essential that plant pot covers should first be placed in the rings into which plant pots are then placed — this will ensure that surplus moisture draining through the soil collects in the bottom of the pot holder and not on the carpet! A further small precaution will be to tip away regularly any water that has accumulated in the outer pot as it is important that plants should not stand in water for any length of time.

Hanging Baskets

You may be keen to grow plants in the house, but feel you cannot because there is insufficient space to accommodate them. The surprising thing is that you often have much more room than you had ever imagined — it's above your head. In every building the largest area of free and unused space is above your head, and it is quite amazing the number of plants and other accessories that the inventive person can suspend from his ceilings.

To suspend the more conventional moss-lined hanging basket from the ceiling indoors would result in an almost continual shower bath, as it is the intention with moss-lined baskets that all surplus moisture should drain through the moss on to the floor below. Out of

doors, where such baskets are mostly put to use, such an arrangement is fine, but continual drips do very little for the living-room carpet! Therefore, you should seek out baskets that are designed with a drip tray attached to the base.

Such baskets are usually made of plastic and on the small side compared to the more conventional wire basket that is moss-lined before soil is inserted. Being much smaller they are obviously not going to hold the same amount of soil, so do not expect the same sort of results. The larger outdoor, or greenhouse-type, basket when filled with soil is quite capable of sustaining a collection of six or more plants for an entire flowering season if feeding is not neglected.

For indoor baskets use a soil that contains a high proportion of peat and restrict the choice of plants to foliage ones rather than flowering types, such as fuchsias and hanging geraniums, both of which require very good light if they are to prosper and retain their flowers. This is not to say, however, that flowering plants are completely taboo, as excellent results can be achieved with baskets filled with columneas or aeschynanthus, provided a reasonable temperature can be maintained.

With the smaller indoor basket the best effect will be had by planting with three or four plants of the same variety, rather than by grouping a collection of different species together. The plants will also be much easier to look after if they all need the same amount of water and fertilizer.

Green foliage plants can have a pleasingly cool appearance when seen suspended from the ceiling, and a fine choice for an individual planting is *Philodendron scandens* with its attractive heart-shaped glossy green leaves, allowed to trail rather than climb. Another that is suitable, provided it is never allowed to dry out, is the Creeping Fig, *Ficus pumila*. Keep it out of sunny windows and away from the drying heat of radiators. For cooler rooms that are well lit there is a wide selection of ivies with both green and variegated foliage. Green leaved ivies will tolerate dark situations and those with smaller leaves are best suited to planting in baskets.

Another good subject for cool, well-lit conditions is the tradescantia of which there are many different forms and colours. Periodic pinching-out of leading shoots will ensure that your basket full of tradescantia plants will retain a pleasing rather than untidy shape. Trailing ferns, such as nephrolepis and *Asparagus densiflorus* as well as trailing peperomias and chlorophytums are also suitable for hanging baskets.

A final word on baskets: the hook securing the basket to the ceiling must be firm enough to support the basket when the soil is wet and the basket is heaviest. And the basket should never be so high on the ceiling that maintainance becomes a problem – suspended just above head height is about right.

Plants as Room Dividers

As room dividers, potted plants offer an excellent alternative to the sort of furniture that is specifically manufactured for this purpose. When plants are used to divide large interiors into sections as, for instance, the living-dining areas, they offer some flexibility, as well as providing privacy without a solid wall.

To facilitate movement of plants, many of the containers that are manufactured specifically as planters have easy running castors fitted to the base of them. Containers of this type, besides being useful for the time when rearrangement of plants is necessary, will also make cleaning a much simpler task.

Containers are available in a wide variety of shapes and sizes, but as room dividers the square or oblong trough types are best, as they

121

can be more easily butted together to form a barrier between one part of the room and the other. Some of the containers are fitted with capillary watering devices which greatly reduce the need for visiting the planters with the watering can, as it is only necessary to top up the water reservoir in the bottom of the container about once every two weeks. However, it must be stressed that the reservoir should be allowed to dry out completely and remain dry for about five days between each topping up operation — this will permit the soil in the container to become aerated, which would be impossible if it remained wet all the time.

Although containers used as room dividers are essentially oblong in shape, there is no reason why the feature should not be made up as a combination of smaller containers. The advantage here is that if several plants are used they can each be planted in their individual boxes, so that any problems that may occur with the soil in the box at a later date will be confined to one container and will not affect all the plants. If preferred, a layer of gravel can be placed in the bottom of the container and the plants, in their pots, placed on this.

In many instances indoors there is often the need for providing a container for a given location and it may then be necessary for one of the correct size to be made. When making such containers it is important that they should not be too unwieldy, so if a very long trough type container is wanted, it may be necessary to build it in two or more sections.

Width and depth are important factors to consider if large plants that are intended to climb to the ceiling are envisaged. Tall plants of 1·8 m (6 ft) or more in height will have to have a considerable bulk of soil around their roots to keep them going. Therefore, it means providing containers large enough to accept pots that may be as much as 25 cm (10 in) in diameter; the trough that is made must be at least that much across. The depth of the pot will be in the region of 30 cm (1 ft), but it would be wiser to allow for at least 38 cm (15 in) in order that a layer of gravel may be placed in the bottom of the trough on which the plant pots can be placed. The container must also have a liner of metal or plastic, so that any surplus moisture gathers in the bottom of the container rather than running out on to the carpet.

Climbing Plants
Having prepared the trough for accommodating the roots of the plant, or the pot, there is then need for providing some form of support on which the chosen plants may be allowed to climb. A simple trellis is probably the best way of overcoming the problem, and it can either have diamond- or square-shaped sections. Most trellis sections that are purchased ready-made for the job are almost invariably a dull brown in colour and not very interesting as features in the home. But the same trellis can be made to look very different simply by painting it white (or a colour that blends with the room's colour scheme) rather than brown, and leaves will be set off much more effectively against the white.

The cheapest method of providing some form of support is to screw a 5 × 2·5 cm (2 × 1 in) slat into the ceiling immediately above the trough, and to insert stout screw eyelets into the slat. It will then be a simple task to tie thick nylon string from the eyelets in the ceiling to similar eyelets screwed into the trough. Screws can be inserted into either side of the trough so that the string can be traced up and down to form an open tent shape up which plant growth can either be trained or allowed to grow naturally. Done in this fashion the growth of the plant will be much less congested and will grow very much better.

By fixing a similar slat to the ceiling, you can employ slender lathes of wood for plants to grow against, the lathes to be pinned to the ceiling slat at one end and to a centre bar of wood running through the length of the trough at the bottom.

Possibly the best plant of climbing habit that is intended for a location offering poor light is the Grape Ivy, *Rhoicissus rhomboidea*, with *Philoden-*

dron scandens running a close second. If rapid growth is an important need in the climbing plant used as a room divider there can be no better choice than *Tetrastigma voinieriana* — a vine that will grow at almost frightening pace if the prevailing conditions are to its liking.

Light
Room dividers are usually some distance from the natural light source of the window, so highly coloured plants such as crotons and variegated plants such as *Hedera canariensis* are comparatively unsuitable as they need ample light to keep them in good condition. Although crotons are not of climbing habit and would not be suitable if a trellis or other framework were used, they could well be included in plant boxes that are raised on a waist-high wall near a window. The advantage of the latter method is that the plants are more easily seen in respect of their

watering and other requirements and can be dealt with without need for too much bending.

If plants are some distance from the natural light source they will benefit from having artificial lighting placed above them, especially during the evening when they will not only benefit growthwise from the additional light but they will also be considerably improved in appearance.

Bottle Gardens
An ideal and novel way to grow plants is in large bottles. The plants give off water vapour while growing, the stopper in the opening of the bottle prevents this escaping, and some goes back into the compost. The air remains as humid as the plants need it.

A bottle garden is a highly attractive arrangement for growing plants. The glass makes the plants look larger than life and the whole scene

BELOW:
Carboys and large bottles can be usefully employed to form micro-environments for groups of plants. Choose plants which are slow growing, and will not invade their neighbours. Once established, the glass container can be positioned prominently in the home, with perhaps the benefit of a light directed on to it.

within the bottle takes on a slightly mysterious and jungle-like appearance. A bottle garden is portable, it doesn't need bright light, the plants look after themselves, more or less, and, once planted, will keep going for years. And in addition, pest troubles are eliminated.

You can use any sort of large bottle which has clear or pale-green glass; carboys with narrow necks and balloon-shaped bodies, of 22·5—45 litres (5—10 gallons) capacity, are the most frequently used, but sweet-jars, hanging plastic or glass bubbles, champagne magnums or chemists' jars can all be pressed into service. In fact, any glass container which can be stoppered can be used for a bottle garden.

The one disadvantage of bottle gardens is the reduction of the available light, so only leafy plants can be grown. There are plenty of low-growing and slow-growing foliage plants and many of them have leaves which are not wholly coloured green.

Choose plants which will not be cramped by the size of the container. Some plants which can be used in bottle gardens are: the small-leaved ivies, the Creeping Fig (*Ficus pumila*), the smaller of the Starfish Bromeliads (Cryptanthus spp.), dwarf dracaenas, *Pilea cadierei* and *P. spruceana*, ferns such as *Pteris cretica* 'Albolineata' or the Maidenhair, tradescantias, the smaller palms such as *Chamaedorea elegans*, fittonia, marantas, *Peperomia caperata*, and any other small bushy plants with ornamental leaves.

When you are about to start planning, don't try to cram the container full straightaway; remember that the plants will grow and gradually fill in spaces between them, and watching the scene change as they do this is half the fun of a bottle garden. Use quite small plants, from 5 cm (2 in) pots; you will find that between five and nine of these will be enough for a carboy, depending on its size. Sweet-jars and wine or champagne bottles will take perhaps four, five or six.

Planting a bottle garden is a fiddly job and you will find it a help, before you start planting, to put the plants on a piece of paper the same size and shape as the base of the container and arrange them in the pattern you prefer. You can see what goes with what, you can contrast or blend colours, and you can fit the creepers in among the bushy plants, with one or two upright kinds to break up the horizontal line. This will also help you to see how many you can grow in your size of container. Remember to choose plants which like the same conditions of warmth, light and moisture. Remember also that glass will make this miniature garden look larger and more beautiful than life, but it will also magnify mistakes in the arrangement.

For the planting you will need: a household fork and spoon, and an empty cotton reel, each bound on to the ends of canes (or the cane can be forced into the hole of the cotton reel), a piece of stout wire with a hook on the end or a pair of long-handled sugar-tongs, a funnel of rolled-up stiff paper, long enough to reach to the bottom of the container, a small piece of sponge also attached to a cane, a child's paintbrush, a length of narrow tubing or an indoor watering-can with a narrow spout, potting compost, gravel or other drainage material, charcoal — which is not essential but good for absorbing impurities — and, of course, the plants.

The compost should be moist, and extra peat mixed into it will make it even more like that found on the forest floor. It must be sterilized to prevent the introduction of fungus disease or weed seeds.

Put in the drainage material first, with charcoal if used, through the funnel, in a layer between 2·5—5 cm (1—2 in) thick, then gently add the moist compost in the same way, and spread it about with the fork so that it is evenly thick, to a depth of 5—10 cm (2—4 in), depending on the container size. Firm it down with the cotton reel. Use the spoon to make the hole for the first plant.

Start with a plant which will be nearest to the wall of the bottle in your design, or at the furthest end, and remove all the compost from its roots. Holding it with the tongs or the wire hook (lightly, otherwise you won't be able to detach it), lower it into the hole in the compost. Pull the compost over the roots with the spoon or fork, and firm it with the cotton reel again, making sure that the plant is upright and the roots spread out as much as you can manage.

Do the same with the other plants, working towards the centre or near-end of the bottle until all are planted.

Then run water at room temperature gently into the bottle, down the sides with the help of the tube or watering-can, until the compost is moist but not saturated. Any extra water cannot drain out as with an ordinary container, though it can collect in the gravel, so if in doubt it is better to put slightly too little than too much.

Watering like this will help to clean the sides of the container, and if any dirt is still left, it can be wiped off with the sponge. The leaves of the plants can be cleaned, if necessary, with the paintbrush. Finally, put the stopper in and put the bottle in a shaded, warm place.

If there is condensation all over the inside of the bottle within the next few days, there is too much water in it, and the stopper should be removed and replaced, if necessary several times during the next few days, until the plants settle down. If there is only a little condensation near the top of the container, you can leave the stopper in; it will clear and even if it does re-form, not to worry, it may do this at intervals. No condensation at all indicates the need to add water.

When you have got the water balance right, the stopper can be left in and the garden left to itself for weeks and even months. Feeding should not be necessary, and watering only occasional if some moisture escapes through the stopper. After about three years, the plants will have outgrown their space, or come to the end of their life, and the garden can be re-made.

Index

ACKNOWLEDGMENTS
The publishers would like to thank the following organisations
and individuals for their kind permission to reproduce the
photographs in this book:
Bernard Alfieri 60 left; A–Z Botanical Collection 25, 43, 48,
64 left, 73 below, 97; Theo Bergström title; John Bethell
119 left; Pat Brindley 6, 14, 15, 31, 69, 73 above, 79
above, 89, 93, 98 below, 108; Connaissance des Art (R.
Guillemot) 117; W. F. Davidson 26 above right, 30 left,
107; J. E. Downward 56, 67; Valerie Finnis 96; Melvin
Grey 9, 11, 33, 62, 118 below right, 122; Susan Griggs
Agency/Michael Boys 49, 118 above left; A. Huxley 36
below, 41, 80; Peter Hunt 88; G. E. Hyde 58 left, 65 right,
76, 83, 85 above, 103 below; Jackson & Perkins 35;
Leslie Johns 70, 112 left and right; D. J. Kesby 61 above;
Bill Mclaughlin 13 below right, 47 below, 66; Marshall-
Cavendish Publications 23; Dr. Gieuseppe Mazza 29, 38-39,
44–45, 47 above, 51, 85 below; John Moss 26 below, 32
above, 34, 38 left, 40 below, 60 right, 65 left, 68 below left,
75 left, 118 above right; N.H.P.A. (N. Docwra) 100–101;
E. A. Over 82 above; Frances Perry 75 right; Wilhelm
Schacht 22; John Sims 30 right, 37, 40 above, 46, 54, 102,
113, 114–115; Harry Smith Collection ends, 3, 21, 27, 28,
36 above, 50 above and below, 53, 57, 58–59, 61 below,
63, 68 above and below right, 71 above and below, 72, 77,
81, 82 left, 91, 94, 95, 98 above, 99, 109, 124; Spectrum
Colour Library 27 above, 32 below, 39, 78, 79 below,
82 right, 86, 87 above and below, 103 left and right;
Violet Stephenson 116; Sutton Seeds 64 right; Syndication
International 118 below left; Elizabeth Whiting 13 above
right, (G. Henderson) 13 above left, (Tim Street-Porter) 12,
(Tubby) 8, 121 above, 123;